Artaud's Theatre of Cruelty

Artaud's Theatre of Cruelty

Albert Bermel

Methuen Drama

3 5 7 9 10 8 6 4

First published in the United States in 1977 by
Taplinger Publishing Co. Inc., New York

First published in the UK in 2001 by
Methuen Publishing Ltd,

Methuen Drama
A & C Black Publishers Ltd
38 Soho Square
London W1D 3HB

Copyright © 1977 & 2001 Albert Bermel

Albert Bermel has asserted his rights under the Copyright, Designs
and Patents Act 1988 to be identified as the author of this work

ISBN 978 0 413 76660 1

A CIP catalogue record for this book is available from the British Library

Typeset by MATS, Southend-on-Sea, Essex

Printed and bound in the UK by MPG Books Ltd, Bodmin, Cornwall

Contents

Preface

Neither Drugs Nor Madness

Anybody who writes at length about Artaud's life will have to discuss his dependence on drugs and his bouts of bizarre behaviour, culminating in the twelve years he spent imprisoned in asylums. This book is not an account of his life, but of his theatre. I have appended a biographical summary, for reference, without relating it causally to his writings. But even if I had attempted a biographical study, I would have put no stock in what seems to me a fairly general assumption made by people who do not admire Artaud: that his addiction and/or insanity rendered him more sensitive, or assisted his imagination, or could have been even partially responsible for the audacity and unorthodoxy of his ideas. Artaud suffered desperately from his addiction and tested many cures; these and his periods of schizophrenia can only have hampered him as he tried to focus his thoughts, manage his life day by day, and articulate and practise the theatre he dreamed of. Coping with the double affliction exhausted him and diverted him from his purposes.

It would be unnecessary to say this if we were not still romantically disposed to looking on madness (whatever madness is) and drug-induced excitement as states of artistic elation. We use the word inspired with a consciousness of its original meaning, possessed by a spirit, preferably a demon, and are haunted by memories of Thomas De Quincey, Sherlock Holmes, and the power-drunk villains of science fiction, not to mention the legends of *poètes maudits.*

These are partisan remarks. If we believed that Artaud had incurred artistic debts to what were evidently grave handicaps, we could not take his writings seriously as proposals; and I have wanted throughout this book to face up to those proposals as products of a mind that was uncommonly, uncannily lucid. We do find, saturating all of Artaud's writings, ecstatic visions of what theatre might be. These visions, rather than any sensible philosophy or single principle, are what has given Artaud a leading place in the theatre of the twentieth century. In France I have even heard him referred to as 'the father of the modern French theatre'. I am not at all sure that there is any one father – André Antoine, Alfred Jarry and Jacques Copeau insist on being reckoned with – but in any case, Artaud's theatrical ideas have caught on, not because he was deranged or stoned on opium, but because they are extraordinary and yet fierce with sanity.

This book is a secondary and tertiary source of data, although I'd like to think the interpretations are first hand.

I am grateful to the authors of the books and articles I have consulted and listed in the bibliography, including the ones I disagree with. I also thank the Research Foundation of the City University of New York for a grant that enabled me to visit Paris at a time when I was strapped for money; the librarians at the Bibliothèque de l'Arsénal and the Bibliothèque Jacques Doucet; the literary adviser at the Odéon National Theatre; Irving Wardle and Caradoc King, who read the first edition and offered suggestions I was glad to incorporate; and friends and relatives in France, England and the US who, in one way or another, made the going easier.

ALBERT BERMEL
New York, 2000

I

Theatre as Therapy

1

The Breakaway

The writings of Artaud give a sympathetic reader the feeling that anything is possible in the theatre. Artaud had passionately committed his life to possibilities – that is, to what other people would consider impossibilities. His poet's cunning and his prophetic fervor continually transform his notations of what ought to be into what is, so that one comes almost to imagine his theatrical visions realized. And yet those visions do not add up to a program or blueprint; there is little point in describing or criticizing them as though they formed a coherent whole. Prophets foresee by lightning flashes and glimmers of light. They do not tell the future, only splinters of it. I suspect that the very notion of a systematic Artaudian theatre would have been abhorrent to Artaud.[1] He knew that every new work of art – a theatrical production of an established play as much as a painting or a novel – means a fresh, painful start. One critic says that 'a study of any single aspect of his work leads only to partial truths since everything he wrote is profoundly interconnected. For example: His concept of the theatre becomes fully comprehensible only after the deep impression made upon him by Surrealism is understood.'[2] I would argue with most of that quotation, beginning with the contradiction in terms, 'partial truths'. To assert that Artaud's writings are 'profoundly interconnected' is to beg a question. How profound is profound and how deeply is it necessary to excavate? This critic does not, could not, come up with Artaud's unitary 'concept of the theatre', let alone render it 'fully comprehensible'. Poetry and prophecy do not offer themselves to full comprehensibility; they call forth individual and varying responses.

One of my own purposes in writing this book was to put

3

stress on the plurality of Artaud's artistry. Unifying it or constricting it into a theory would do it an injustice.[3] A theory implies limitations of some kind; Artaud's writings evince a hatred for limitations, especially conventional ones. By contrast, a theatre of possibilities glories in the absence of limitations; its soil is the untilled future. Insofar as there is a critical framework in this book it is mine, not Artaud's.

His best-known publication, *The Theatre and Its Double*,[4] which appeared in English less than twenty years ago, consists of a preface, ten essays (most of them originally given as lectures), seven letters and two 'notes', a gathering that does not have an inevitable sequence and is far from being a sustained argument or a book; rather, it resembles in format those collections of columns by reviewers that bunch up their opinions under some noncommittal but catchy title. As it happens, the recovery of Artaud's writings is still under way in France.[5] What we call his works, then, is a large number of fragments; in turn these fragments are urgently suggestive, not ordered in a formally correct manner, for Artaud had no use for accepted forms; they distract the theatre from its true artistic ends. 'If there is still one hellish, truly accursed thing in our time, it is our artistic dallying with forms, instead of being like victims burnt at the stake, signaling through the flames.'[6]

To tell us how a European play from the distant past was performed we have only skimpy information to draw on.[7] Whether it be a Greek tragedy two and a half millennia old, a Roman comedy or tragedy by Plautus, Terence, or Seneca, which is two thousand years away from us, a medieval play cycle, a Spanish *capa y espada* adventure, or an Elizabethan-Jacobean epic from the sixteenth or seventeenth century, we must rely on unreliable data and speculation supplied by some historians and challenged by others. And we must scrutinize the dramatic text. Often the texts of long-lived plays are themselves questionable, they have passed through so many hands, some of which may have remodelled them or made 'improvements'. But a director embarking on a production of, say, a tragedy by Euripides can resolve the textual questions to his satisfaction much more comfortably than he can decide on a style for his show. Shall it, for example, reflect the habits, behaviour and attitudes of the citizens of ancient Athens, insofar as these are known? Or should it say something about the society in which he and his audiences live? Or can he exploit both of these periods at the same time? And then, what sort of lighting, costumes, stage compositions, movements, speech and scenery will result from his decisions? What moods will he seek to establish, since some tragedies by Euripides are more tragic than others, and even the grimmest of them contain episodes that undercut the tragic tone?

Now, the text, even if corrupt in places, is already there, its authority certified by its having been printed and by its tangibility as an object. But in addition, the text of a play that is old is literature and therefore worthy of respect, if not awe. In the late 1920s and early 1930s when Artaud was active in the theatre 'reverence for the text', as Jacques Copeau had called it, remained an ideal in revivals of the classics by directors like Charles Dullin and Louis Jouvet who had both belonged to Copeau's troupe, the Vieux Colombier, and with both of whom Artaud worked. Few directors of the time would risk the wrath of purists among the reviewers (or the purist in each of themselves) by drastically cutting lines or characters or by rearranging the sequence of dramatic events; when they did make minor alterations they wanted to simplify the play for the audience, or make it less tedious, or censor material they thought raw or excessive; rarely did they reshape the play so as to make a new entity out of it. The upshot of all this reverence was that one revival of *Hamlet* or *Antigone* looked and sounded as neo-Victorian as any other. The personality of a leading performer might add some novelty so that the production could be named after his or her interpretation, much as in the eighteenth and nineteenth centuries (Edmund Kean's Iago, Mrs Siddons's Lady Macbeth, Talma's Hamlet, Salvini's Othello), but the directors' contributions usually differed from one another only superficially: they were meek tamperings, not real innovations.

Or so it seemed to Artaud. He was disgusted to his fibres with the theatre he saw in Paris and knew of elsewhere.[8] The commercial staging had become 'an inferior art, a means of popular distraction', and 'an outlet for our worst instincts'. It consisted of 'falsehood and illusion', such as 'stories about money, worry over money, social careerism, the pangs of love unspoiled by altruism, sexuality sugar-coated with an eroticism that [had] lost its mystery ... torments, seductions and lusts before which we are nothing but Peeping Toms gratifying our cravings'. The established masterpieces, on the other hand, which were thought to set the standards or tone for all theatre, were 'literary, that is to say, fixed; and fixed in forms that no longer respond to the needs of the time'. What Artaud called 'the idolatry of fixed masterpieces' was 'one of the aspects of bourgeois conformism', which in turn led to the nurturing by theatre practitioners of 'snobbish, precious, aesthetic mentalities which the public does not understand'. The theatre's 'veneration for what has already been created', according to Artaud, 'petrifies us' and 'deadens our responses'.

In other words, 'masterpieces of the past are good for the past: they are not good for us.' Their 'grand notions' might well have an effect on the public, but only so long as the public was 'addressed in its own language', and not subjected to 'adulterated trappings and speech that belong to extinct eras'. Artaud believed that the contemporary theatre, especially in its staging of the classics, should employ means that were 'immediate and direct, corresponding to present modes of feeling, and understandable to everyone', as well as being in consonance with 'the rude and epileptic rhythm of our time'.[9]

The kind of theatre Artaud envisaged would use the classics but only after subjecting them to a radical overhaul. Lighting, sound equipment and other technical means would no longer subserve the text; they would partially replace it. The noises, music and colours that generally accompany the lines would in places substitute for them. They would be fortified by a range of human noises – screams, grunts, moans, sighs, yelps – together with a repertoire of gestures, signs and other movements. These would extend the range of the actor's art and the receptivity of the spectator. To put it another way, they would enlarge the theatre's vocabulary. It might then deal more comprehensively than ever before with irrational states of being and understanding. Through the new acting and directing techniques the unconscious minds of the director and actors would speak to the unconscious mind of each spectator.

Artaud's assumption here seems to be that rational communication is theatrically limited, if not played out. In a debate, two characters with opposing views marshal their points into a logic that is carefully prepared for them by the playwright and developed in a rhetorical pattern. Their dialogue engages the spectator by swaying his conscious mind, especially his intellect, first in one direction, then in another. One character, let us say, is arguing in favour of tyranny, the other in favour of democracy. The spectator listens and decides that one case is stronger or more appealing than the other, or perhaps he cannot decide which speaker is right. Or while he approves of democracy in principle, he finds the character who supports tyranny more eloquent or more sympathetic as a personality. Such debates belong to the traditional western form of dramatic dialectic which comes down to us from Athenian civilization. We take note, and then take sides according as we are won over. Even if we find it hard to make a decision we still judge on the basis of our intellects and our conscious feelings.

Artaud did not care whether his characters won or lost arguments. He wanted to use them in order to expose his audiences to a range of their own feelings that was unconscious and therefore normally inaccessible to them. They would surrender themselves to a performance, live through it and feel it, rather than merely think about it. More than seven centuries ago Roger Bacon differentiated between two 'modes of knowing', experience and argument. For Artaud the average performance has too much argument in it and too little – if any – experience. But why should he have believed that in the theatre experience and feeling are more desirable than argument and thought? And why should he emphasize the irrational elements in theatre at the expense of the rational? To deal with these questions we can begin by looking into his convictions – obsessive in their intensity – about the relationships between society and the theatre, or more broadly, how the theatre can discover what he called the 'passionate equation between Man, Society, Nature, and Objects'.

CHAPTER 1: THE BREAKAWAY

1. Artaud's observations apropos of the philosophy of Maurice Maeterlinck could be applied to his own work: 'In no way does it constitute a system. It has no architecture or form, only size, height, and density.' (*Collected Works*, Vol. 1, p. 240.)
2. Naomi Greene, *Antonin Artaud: Poet Without Words*, p. 56.
3. Artaud found a single name for his theatrical ideals, the Theatre of Cruelty, but he arrived at it after long meditation, and it is poetic shorthand, not realistic description.
4. Antonin Artaud, *The Theatre and Its Double*, trans. Mary Caroline Richards (New York: Grove Press, 1958).
5. A 'new, revised, and corrected' edition of the *Complete Works* in French is now superseding the former edition (*Antonin Artaud: Oeuvres Complètes*). This is, so to speak, the 'completer' works. Further research will undoubtedly turn up more letters and possibly more unpublished essays and lost plays.
6. Artaud, *The Theatre and Its Double*, p. 13.
7. The better known oriental theatres, in contrast with the European ones, have a nearly unbroken tradition of acting and plenty of documentary material to hand in the form of such guides as the *Natyashastra* for Sanskrit drama, written about 2,000 years ago by the sage Bharata Muni, and Zeami Motokiyo's detailed notes on the Noh drama, which date back to the early fifteenth century.
8. With, naturally, a few exceptions, such as the French experiments in Surrealism, with which Artaud was associated early in his career, and the innovations tried by Vsevolod Meyerhold, Evgeny Vakhtangov and Aleksandr Tairov in Russia.
9. Quotations from essay 'No More Masterpieces', *The Theatre and Its Double*, pp. 74–78.

2

Redefinitions

Artaud's essay 'The Theatre and the Plague' amazingly proposes that one of the great scourges of mankind, the plague, in many ways resembles the theatre which, as an art, consists of some of mankind's great acts of affirmation. He opens the essay with an account of a nightmare suffered in 1720 by a Viceroy of Sardinia, who dreams his community is consumed by the plague. As a result of the nightmare he later forbids a passing ship to dock at the Sardinian harbour of Caligari. The Viceroy's order is 'considered irresponsible, absurd, idiotic, and despotic by the public and by his own staff'. But he insists. The ship has to sail on and dock at Marseille where it unleashes the devastating epidemic of 1720. How does one explain the Viceroy's oracular dream? Artaud says that there seems to have been a 'palpable communication, however subtle' between him and the plague, anything but the usual 'contagion by contact'.

In narrating the Viceroy's dream, and in the same essay, describing the characteristics of history's worst plagues, Artaud identifies the disease's ravaging of the human body with the disintegration of a plague-ridden society. Much as a plague victim's body refuses to obey his brain, so all forms of public administration and communication in the state break down. Fleshy matter turns inert, into stone, into powder-like substances, and these clog the body's channels, while corpses litter the streets, too many of them to burn in the pyres that are 'lit at random'. The victims and survivors, in a condition of mixed panic and delirium, behave crazily against the grain in an orgy of 'gratuitous absurdity', as though released from all social conventions and sanctions:

The obedient and virtuous son kills his father; the chaste man performs sodomy upon his neighbors. The lecher becomes pure. The miser throws his gold in handfuls out the window. The warrior hero sets fire to the city he once risked his life to save.

Artaud similarly links the processes of bodily degeneration with the 'natural' damage done to landscapes by storms and gigantic earth movements. He compares the body fluids with 'lava kneaded by subterranean forces' seeking an outlet, and skin blisters and their outer circles with Saturn surrounded by its rings of vapour. The body is a society, is a planet. Not content with these leaps of the imagination, Artaud goes on to draw analogies between a victim of the plague and an actor or a playwright, and then between an actor and a murderer. He does not prove these analogies, he asserts them. The reader in his turn does not deduce them or find flaws in Artaud's reasoning, because there is no reasoning: one rejects the correspondences outright, or one accepts them, at least provisionally, by submitting to the dramatic and poetic power of Artaud's prose. This prose, like the theatre Artaud wanted to bring to birth, is itself a kind of experience that speaks to the unconscious and the senses, not to common sense.

It evokes the plague as a time of delirium, a delirium which, like theatre, is 'communicative'; as a time of 'immense liquidation', when the sickness and its aftermath wantonly destroy; and as a time of 'extremity' which, again like theatre, calls forth exaggerated gestures that will release unsuspected passions, including repressed and forbidden sexual desires. Both theatre and the plague need a language of symbols and archetypes to do them justice. Both reveal 'a depth of latent cruelty [in men and nature] by means of which all the perverse possibilities of the mind, whether of an individual or a people, are localized'. Artaud conceives that at the time of plague 'there is a kind of strange sun, a light of abnormal intensity', under which 'the difficult and even the impossible suddenly become our normal element'.

Artaud's aim in this essay is in truth to laud the plague's effects. If it wrecks 'our present social state', so much the better;

that state is 'iniquitous'. The plague is an inescapable calamity in the cycle of man's history, a 'triumph of dark powers', and a 'total crisis'; but after it has struck and then exhausted itself 'nothing remains except death or an extreme purification', for 'a gigantic abscess, as much moral as social, has been collectively drained'.[1] The plague, in a word, cleanses. Like a boil it brings whatever would have remained noxious, hidden and festering to the surface – and expels it. Theatre can do likewise. It simulates the dark, unindulged passions, the abnormal feelings, of mankind (the actor is a murderer) and, by expelling them at one remove, in performance, cleanses the performer and spectator alike in its collective experience.

Twenty-three hundred years earlier Aristotle had viewed theatre as an act of purgation, catharsis. But Artaud goes much further than Aristotle went. Rather than concurring that theatre is a healthy diversion to be described by such adjectives as 'pleasant, entertaining, enjoyable', he insists – and is the first writer to do so – that it is, like the plague, a social necessity.

If theatre is a necessary part of our lives, an activity we cannot forgo without suffering the consequences, it has a 'true destiny' that is much more momentous than dabbling in safe formulas that cause its audiences to smile, weep, frown, shudder and remain unchanged. It has an obligation: its every performance must, by virtue of its cleansing and purifying, transfigure those audiences. They must be, and feel, remade. Artaud employs three images that relate to this transfiguration: those of alchemy, metaphysics and culture.

Much as Francis Bacon defended alchemy on the grounds that 'the search and endeavours to make gold have brought many useful inventions and instructive experiments to light', so Artaud viewed alchemy as a great spiritual aspiration, a yearning to 'rediscover in solid and opaque form the expression of light itself, of rarity, and of irreducibility'. Gold, cleansed of its impurities in the normal processes of refining, comes about by a mere chemical reduction. But the gold dreamed of at the end of the alchemist's rainbow is a noble vision born out of a hope of transforming other material substances and out of a

11

'nostalgia for pure beauty'. Alchemy is 'the spiritual double' of chemistry, much as the theatre Artaud dreams of is the spiritual double of the impoverished theatre that exists in his time, not a 'mere inert replica' of banal reality, but a double of 'another archetypal and dangerous reality' which never shows itself plainly. Further, he observes that books on alchemy have 'a curious predilection for the theatrical vocabulary . . . as if their authors had sensed from the beginning all that was *representative*, i.e. theatrical' in alchemy's strivings for the metal of metals. In a similar fashion the theatre's constant distilling and experiments can lead to 'the alchemical theatre', that mirage-like performance of performances.

Artaud's understanding of the word metaphysics has an affinity with the meanings he attaches to alchemy. Metaphysics does not serve him as a synonym for abstruse philosophical speculation, but suggests a type of artistic investigation that goes literally beyond the physical or outward limits of the art and into its virtuality, or what it is capable of becoming. 'True poetry' is metaphysical and 'true theatre' depends on this poetry by exploiting all the theatre's means, not merely words. Staging is a 'language in space and movement', a language of signs and hieroglyphs that 'struggles directly with the stage without passing through words', for words with their circumscribed denotations are 'Occidental' or 'Latin' or 'pig-headed', instead of being 'active and anarchic', as they become when they produce musical or surprising effects as sounds. What does the noun tree tell us about a tree? It echoes an association: the association is stale and therefore obvious, and 'obvious ideas are, in theatre, as everywhere else, dead and done with'. One might say they are no longer ideas, but habits, the sloughed-off skins of ideas. Yet the word tree does have a sound in its own right, just as a tree has an identity that is independent of its name. The sound of tree, when divorced from the association, and when spoken in varied ways for its sonority, carries a range of new associations for a listener, depending on how the word is uttered.

Artaud says that a metaphysical language consisting of gestures, signs, attitudes, stage sets, objects, movements, and a speech pattern of word-sounds and other sounds – all of it amounting to incantation – will help us to find again the 'religious and mystic preference' of which our theatre has lost the original sense because of its servitude to psychology and 'human interest'. It will release us from the repetitions, in theatre as in life, of 'accessible everyday experience', and plunge us back into the very origins of theatre and the needs from which it sprang.

In so doing, theatre will serve as the entrance into our culture. The word culture has two principal usages, and Artaud vehemently distinguishes them. The first designates those arts and manners (or mannerisms) that appeal to a favoured segment of a population, people we sarcastically refer to today as the élite or – if they make a fetish out of belonging to the segment – as élitists. Artaud has contempt for this culture, especially when the word comes from the mouths and pens of men who take upon themselves the task of becoming its guardians and interpreters, the same ones, doubtless, who venerate masterpieces and complain about the weakening of traditional values and the decline of craftsmanship. Paradoxically, these are the same men who, as apologists for industrial civilization, point to culture as an affirmation of their superiority over their forebears. This species of culture accumulates: the more of it there is on display, the more positive they can feel about their superiority. The idea that culture is no more than this accumulation of artifacts is, says Artaud, 'a lazy, unserviceable notion which engenders an imminent death'. Perhaps he means here that the growing pile of this inert culture, like slag, will soon bury us; it is esteemed for 'the profits we seek to derive from it'. A phenomenon distinct from life, it is praised 'as if there were culture on one side and life on the other'.

The second usage, which he automatically labels 'true culture', is, by contrast, 'a refined means of understanding and *exercising* life'. It comes close in meaning to the usage by anthropologists and sociologists today, and encompasses all the arts of living practised by everybody in a society. But Artaud is talking about a pre-industrial, non-civilized society, for this true culture 'relies upon the barbaric and primitive means of totemism whose savage, i.e. entirely spontaneous, life I wish to worship'. Among the Mexican Indians, for example, 'there is no art: things are made for use. And the world is in perpetual exaltation.'[2]

Cleansing, transfiguration, exaltation – these are objectives Artaud will accomplish through the medium of 'cruelty'. The word cruelty came in for plenty of criticism after he had fastened on to it as a summation of the theatre he would come to practise in the mid-1930s, and even more after he named his short-lived company the Theatre of Cruelty. It seemed to some of his friends that cruelty sounded restrictive. It did not conjure up for them the broad and ambitious programme he was striving for, nor did it sound inviting. What could a theatre of cruelty stand for other than punishment for the spectator? Artaud defended the term hotly and often, supplementing it with other words such as terror, violence and danger. He did appear to intend that a punishment of a sort be visited on spectators. However, it would be a beneficent punishment. Life has in it a lot of ugliness and evil, which are both natural and man-made. Instead of shielding spectators from their impact he would expose them, put them through the experience of a danger and then free them from it. He went to great pains to explain that his theatre was not a form of torture, but a facing of the worst that could happen, followed by a refreshing release from it. At the end the spectator would feel relieved, as if awakening from a nightmare, the evil and terror cleansed away.

Artaud claimed that the theatre lacked patrons because it did not cope with the anguish that is common to all men, with the extreme desires and fears that haunt man's dreams and are therefore an integral part of his inner reality. Audiences turned to films, the circus, spectator sports and newspaper reports of calamities and disasters for their 'violent satisfactions'. The theatre should provide, but did not, plenty of 'immediate and violent action', so that it was not outplayed by the violence and immediacy of life itself. Its fictions should be stranger than truth.

Artaud's Theatre of Cruelty would tackle 'famous

personages, atrocious crimes, superhuman devotions', and treat of these subjects so as to relate them to 'the terrible lyricism' of the great myths of mankind, most of which have dealt with defiance of social and ethical norms. The 'image of crime', as presented in a purely theatrical way, he asserted, is 'something infinitely more terrible for the spirit than that same crime when actually committed'.

There are thus three outstanding features of the Theatre of Cruelty as Artaud projects it in theory. First, it does not involve physical or spiritual maltreatment; rather, it artistically expresses what he calls in different places the rigour or necessity or implacability of life. Second, this theatre draws on the individual dreams and the collective dreams, or the myths, of all men. It will furnish each spectator with 'the truthful precipitates of dreams, in which his taste for crime, his erotic obsessions, his savagery, his chimeras, his utopian sense of life and matter, even his cannibalism, pour out, on a level not counterfeit and illusory, but interior'. Third, because it works on the nerves and senses, rather than on the intellect, and because it impinges on anxieties common to all men, the Theatre of Cruelty is aimed at a general public, not the usual run of theatregoers only. Whether they realize it or not, the poetic state of feeling such a theatre arouses is 'a transcendent experience of life' for everybody, life lived more passionately for the duration of a performance, and this experience, if withheld, will be sought more brutally in 'crime, drugs, war, or insurrection'.[3]

The Balinese theatre, which Artaud encountered during its visits to France, the first time in Marseille and eight years later in Paris, kindled his imagination. His two essays, 'On the Balinese Theatre' and 'Oriental and Occidental Theatre', illustrate not only a number of ideals that animate and tantalize him, but also the difficulty of paraphrasing his writing. His thoughts fly about and glance off one another, criss-crossing many ideas in his other published documents, but always remaining airborne, as he struggles to shape obdurate words into his visionary theatre. He believes simultaneously that this

15

theatre is ineffable and that he can, indeed must, convey its essence. His direct source of reference, if not inspiration, is the Balinese theatre, a combination of dance, song, pantomime and sound, which he had seen in Paris. Much of what he says about this spectacle applies to other forms of oriental theatre, too, say the Sanskrit, the Noh, Kabuki and Peking Opera.

He makes no attempt to describe it systematically; rather, he provides glimpses of startling moments and states of being and feeling: a repeated gesture of a performer's right hand touching his head 'as if wishing to indicate the position and existence of some unimaginable central eye, some intellectual egg'; the 'banked luminous circles' of women's feathered headdresses; the folds of robes which, 'curving above the buttocks, hold them as if suspended in air' and prolong a dancer's leap into a 'flight'; the 'mechanically rolling eyes, pouting lips, and muscular spasms'.

Over the centuries the forms of this dance-theatre have grown fixed and conventionalized;[4] they now have acquired a mathematical precision which produces 'methodically calculated effects', devoid of spontaneity. Like any severely disciplined performers, the members of the Balinese troupe hold fast to their range of activities, yet can float spiritually free of it. They govern it and it governs them, and at the same time it liberates them. At this height of accomplishment there is a mystical tone to the performance and it is precisely this mysticism that fascinates Artaud.

For the word mysticism, as for cruelty, he has a compendium of synonyms and near-synonyms. He writes of magic, sorcery, miracles, of the divine and the marvellous. He admires in the Balinese their ability to reach a state of ecstasy, delirium, intoxication, trance, and to propel their audiences into this same mood of spellbound alertness, a mood one might sum up by imagining oneself awake during a dream. The dreamer is caught up, enchanted by the dream. It is happening to him but he is aware that it is happening and can virtually stand outside the dream and observe himself in it.

The Balinese achieve this result by having invented and become masters of a language that is 'pure theatre', a 'language without meaning except in the circumstances of the stage'. This language goes far beyond ordinary dialogue, which is 'logical' and 'discursive'. It depends on mime and movement, on space, on the imaginary network of lines traced by a step, an arm gesture, or a nod. These physical activities have no relationship to the body's everyday, utilitarian movements. If the western theatre imitates life, Artaud might say, the oriental theatre creates its own life. It has found a speech that is prior to words. Nor is it purely emotional. It has an intellectual component, which he contrasts with the intellectuality of western plays. The latter seek to define the thoughts of the playwright, the former, to 'cause thinking' by the audience, and complicated thinking at that. It 'sets up vibrations, not on a single level [following what is going on in the drama], but on every level of the mind at once'. In its fixedness and its power to evoke wonder, it has affinities with a religious ceremony, a rite. And, like a rite, it can be participated in by anybody, not just a select group of the brightest or best-informed people. It is popular theatre.

Here I should drop a reminder that we are talking not about what the Balinese performance objectively is, but how Artaud interprets it. Anything but a textbook scholar, he responds to it with his heart and nerves as an awesomely receptive spectator. At the same time, in reflecting on its precision, its beauties, its mystical and incantatory powers, its popular appeal to Balinese audiences, and its mental and emotional stimuli, he is brooding about what he can take from it to convert to his own ends. The oriental theatre he writes of is not only what Artaud sees; it is what he wishes to see. And to borrow.[5]

CHAPTER 2: REDEFINITIONS

1. Quotations from essays 'The Theatre and the Plague' and 'Metaphysics and the *Mise en Scène*', *The Theatre and Its Double*, pp. 15–47.
2. Quotations from different essays, *The Theatre and Its Double*; most from 'The Theatre and Culture', pp. 7–13, and 'The Alchemical Theatre', pp. 48–52.

17

3. Quotations from essays 'No More Masterpieces' and 'The Theatre and Cruelty', *The Theatre and Its Double*, pp. 74–88.

4. This is true of all traditional theatres, even the most recently born, the Kabuki. Naturally, the performance changes slightly according to the gifts of the individual dancers, but oriental theatre has remained surprisingly stable in its enactment.

5. Quotations from essays 'On the Balinese Theatre', pp. 55–67, and 'Oriental and Occidental Theatre', pp. 68–73, *The Theatre and Its Double*.

3

Inspiration and Aspirations

In the oriental theatre, as in all oriental art, the guiding principle is a quest for unification. The artists forge this unity out of diverse elements; opposites clash and resolve themselves into a oneness, as occurs in life. The very cosmos came out of chaos; warring parts expended their strength and merged into a single entity, and oriental art presents its versions of this merging.

The finest expression of the unification is found in the images of Shiva in his incarnation as Nataraj, the patron god of the Indian dancer and actor. All four classical Indian dances imitate, and are performed in tribute to, the god. He poses with his left leg and foot raised in abandon, while his right foot crushes a little demon. His eyes are closed in ecstasy. One of his four hands (two arms sprout from either shoulder) holds a tiny drum, which resembles a finger-clacker, a second holds fire, 'the purifier and destroyer of evil'. The third hand points upward to show that the god fears nothing. The fourth hand points downward, not to show that he does, after all, fear something – the image is a symbol, not a literal device – but to depict his protection of the world and his gift of bliss to all people. On bronze statues of the god in the temples of southern India he is often enclosed by a ring of fire, the cosmos he created.

The ideal of unification is by no means exclusively oriental. Hegel's thesis and antithesis, which give rise to a synthesis, and Herbert Spencer's cyclical theory of evolution (instability/equilibration/dissolution) are reminiscent of it. But western philosophy and western art do not as a rule observe unification as a final principle, nor acknowledge that it may arouse a state of surpassing joy. The nearest artistic equivalent we have is the tendency toward stability in, for example, Greek and Roman comedies, later formalized in the familiar pattern of the well-made play (stasis/complications/resolution), or in the Elizabethan and Jacobean theatre, the re-establishment of order, frequently brought about by a 'ranking figure'.[1]

Artaud sometimes openly propounds unification as a theatrical end, but it is implicit in almost everything he writes. When, for instance, he mentions the 'great social upheavals, conflicts between people and races, natural forces, interventions of chance, and the magnetism of fatality' as subjects for his Theatre of Cruelty, he seems unconsciously to be thinking beyond the conflicts to their subsidence. The idea consciously surfaces when he writes that true theatre is 'born out of a kind of organized anarchy after philosophical battles which are the passionate aspect of these primitive unifications', the 'unifications' being almost predestined. And again it appears when he conceives of 'conjunctions unimaginably strange to our waking minds', which will 'annihilate every conflict produced by the antagonism of matter and mind, idea and form, concrete and abstract'. He is writing here of the effects that must have proceeded from the Greek Eleusinian Mysteries; he connects them with the ideal of alchemy when he says that they 'must have been the equivalent of spiritualized gold'. In much the same way, the theatre 'language' he dreams of comes out of a unification of such different constituents as sound, gesture and the exploitation of space.[2]

The instrument to provoke and organize the unifying will be the director. In the Balinese theatre, as in the Sanskrit, the director has a long history. He has become a 'kind of manager of magic, a master of sacred ceremonies. And the material on which he works, the themes he brings to throbbing life, are derived not from him but from the gods.' The Balinese director, then, stands in for the gods. He might be regarded as being their priest-interpreter, a Hermes-plus-Tiresias; who plans and arranges the quasi-religious service but does not take part in its enactment.

In Europe the director dates back hardly more than a century, but in that relatively brief span he has grown into a figure of critical importance in revitalizing the classics and inducing playwrights to produce new works by providing them with a house and a company. Artaud, like Gordon Craig, wishes to enlarge the director's function even more: he would elbow the playwright and scenic designer aside and either supply his own original textual material and settings, or adapt earlier writings, however he saw fit, to his own conception of a playing space.

Artaud's yearning to impose a unity on each performance by making the director into a manager marks a culmination of the third phase of western theatre. In the earliest phase the playwright was the manager – in, say, the Athenian theatre, the Elizabethan and in Molière's troupe the company existed to realize his text. In the second phase the actor became a manager and his company came into being primarily to serve as a foil for the acting of his leading lady and himself. Third, the director was to be the centre and unifier and yet to remain outside the actual performance. He was a creator-god. Artaud, however, would claim to be swinging the wheel full circle; not lending impetus to a third phase, but restoring a preliminary phase, one that antedates the Greek playwrights. He hopes to revive an Orphic or Eleusinian idea of sacred theatre, a communal experience to dwarf a modern drama that consists of little more than the psychological histories of individuals.

Unifying means making whole, or more accurately, realizing a wholeness that was not there before and may even prove to be a revelation. Wholeness, in turn, presupposes health, in the sense of completeness, and the unification Artaud seeks can legitimately be considered as health-giving. The Theatre of Cruelty will promote wholeness and healthiness in the individual theatregoer. Then by bringing him and others together as an audience, it will promote the larger wholeness and health, a feeling of community, in the group. This therapy is an intended consequence of Artaudian theatre, unlike, say, a healthy belly laugh or a good cry in the conventional theatre, which is more like a side effect or an accidental by-product. 'True theatre' is spiritual healing. It enables us to recover 'those

21

energies which ultimately create order and increase the value of life'. Artaud proposes to reintroduce an 'elementary magical idea', adopted by twentieth-century psychoanalysis, which cures a patient 'by making him assume the apparent and exterior attitudes of the desired condition'.

Here, through abreaction, is the strongest justification Artaud can offer for his theories, since healing constitutes the most daring of the possibilities that theatre might fulfil. It helps us to see that Artaud's word cruelty means having to be cruel to be kind. It throws light on his view of masterpieces as a theatrical plague, a curse, and the plague itself as a warning, a blessing in disguise, an inchoate attempt by implacable natural forces to drain away accumulated violence and antisocial behaviour. Finally, healing as purification, as social necessity and as alchemy gives the director-priest an added function: he becomes a medicine man, possibly a doctor. As for the spectator who has experienced an Artaudian performance, witnessed the repressed 'movements of his thought', and seen them theatrically 'illuminated in extraordinary deeds' – with the violence and bloodshed subordinated to the thought – 'I defy that spectator,' writes Artaud, 'to give himself up, once outside the theatre, to ideas of war, riot, and blatant murder.' The cast and director join forces and turn themselves into a collective scapegoat, a revival of the poor man who volunteered to absorb all the evils in a community and then to be exiled or killed. Sir James Frazer tells us in *The Golden Bough* that such a scapegoating took place in antiquity in Artaud's hometown of Marseille, 'one of the busiest and most brilliant of Greek colonies, whenever the plague came'.

We might, then, sum up Artaud's theories as follows: His apparent contempt for the meaningful spoken word, and his extravagant ambitions for non-verbal theatre – lighting, sounds, music, masks, make-up and gesture – in an unorthodox playing space, belong to his effort to find or manufacture a vocabulary of living images that will be intrinsically theatrical; it cannot be put out on loan to such pure literature as poetry and fiction. This new vocabulary of Cruelty communicates by means akin to physical sensation, theatrical 'suffering' or 'pain'. It will

22

allow theatre to mime cosmic and supernatural forces, and to relate man to the entire universe, and to his own history. For Artaud theatre is sacred, an institution for accomplishing self-renewal. A performance can inculcate an experience of oneness, forge a temporary community out of strangers, and play out their interdependence. No other art can quite do this, for theatre takes a congregation of people through adventures – storms, earthquakes, floods, the plague, love, hatred and death, but all by proxy – and brings them out safe. Together they have undergone risks, mended chaos, passed the initiatory trials, and come through whole and healed. Such a theatre will resolve itself into a tribal communion, a cleansing ritual that magically induces peace of mind.

The vision is noble. As I have developed it here it also appears selfless, if not impersonal. There remains the question of whether one relates it to Artaud himself.

Most of Artaud's writings allude directly and symbolically to his own life and plight. But, if I may sound a cautionary note, Artaud's life does not explain his writings; one should distrust criticism about him, or any other artist, that is psychologically deterministic. That Artaud was an invalid for most of his life has some bearing but it does not entirely account for his conception of a theatre that would heal, otherwise any invalid might have conceived the Theatre of Cruelty.

Nevertheless, his temperament does enter into any reckoning with his writing. His exceptional touchiness caused him to feel left out, or shut out, or unjustly criticized, and it lends a unique ardour to his criticism. His fondness for taking extreme positions, his hatred of the commercial theatre and his talent for invective aroused opposition from people who may have felt threatened by his proposals as many still do. Artaud's sense of isolation, even among his friends and well-wishers, often made him reiterate his ideas with a fervour that bordered on the maledictory. As a result, he seemed progressively to become more of a loner and, as he thought, a victim.

It was not easy to remain one of his friends, as is revealed by his correspondence, most notably that of the period 1929 to

1933 after his Théâtre Alfred Jarry had been forced to discontinue for want of funds. His letters to Mme Yvonne Allendy, for example, are full of requests, instructions and demands for 'urgent' or 'immediate' action. He presses her time and again to intercede with patrons, editors, copyright holders; to secure him financial aid, send him books, find him parts in films, to clear rights for him, and dash off letters on his behalf. He reproaches her for her 'annoyance' with him. He assails her with distressing bulletins on the state of his health and feelings. In one express letter to Mme Allendy he dictates the wording of a message-cum-job résumé to be forwarded to Filippo Marinetti, the Italian fascist poet, filmmaker, and founder of the Futurist movement. She is to write this letter immediately. He is 'most eager' to have it 'posted tonight'.

The unhesitating loyalty of his friends appears today as clairvoyance. The people who stood by him were convinced that his gifts would justify their efforts. He realized that his claims on others could be trying, to put it mildly, and frequently apologized for them – before claiming more. Artaud's battles with despair and lack of recognition, although not unlike the survival procedures most artists must endure, were made particularly exhausting by onslaughts of pain and physical debility.

Like most adventurers in the arts he needed the approval of backers for whose taste he had contempt. Possibly out of pride because he could not point back to undoubted successes in his past, and possibly out of self-protection because he could not bring himself to defend such conventional successes in the first place, he often tried to make his friends into intermediaries, if not buffers, between himself and the providers of assets. To complicate his life further, he was torn between three objectives: he had no regular income and hoped to pay his way by doing temporary chores in films and theatre; he wanted to be a poet, critic and fount of manifestos – a force in the literary world; and he dreamed of becoming an artistic mastermind, an independent producer-writer-director-star. He was to touch this last ambition, a Chaplinesque or Molièresque ideal of unification, only once, with his Theatre of Cruelty production

24

of *The Cenci* in 1935, and then to endure a crushing disappointment at its reception.

Artaud's letters show us a frantic, penniless, ailing entrepreneur who soars from paranoia to childlike trustfulness, and slumps from determination to be a winner into reluctance to cast his pearls before swine. We can pick up further clues to his temperament and urticating social attitudes from the events in his life and from the themes that obtrude in his poems, plays, quasi-historical character studies and scenarios.

He writes about copulation more shockingly than does any author before him. In his descriptions the sexual act is almost always warped or perverted, made repellent and feverishly anti-pornographic. In Artaud's fictional worlds we find anything but a parity between spiritual and sexual love. His lovers are antagonists who surrender to a maleficent force. The medieval-to-Victorian idea of sex was that it violated the woman; in Artaud it damages the man. He may risk castration, even. In writing of the lovemaking between Abelard and Héloise Artaud says that Héloise 'had this thing like a sheathed sword', and in his far-from-historical account it is Héloise herself, not her avenging uncle, who mutilates Abelard. But many of Artaud's male figures are brutal, too. Count Cenci, Heliogabalus, Ambrosio in the translation of Matthew Lewis's *The Monk*, and a number of men in the film scenarios perform sadistic acts upon women. Sometimes the lovemaking is incestuous. Cenci rapes his daughter, Heliogabalus fornicates with his mother, the Boy in *The Fountain of Blood* and Ambrosio with their sisters, albeit unknowingly. Artaud wholeheartedly admired John Ford's play *'Tis Pity She's a Whore*, the main plot of which consists in a passionate, lethal affair between Giovanni and his sister Annabella. Heliogabalus also goes in for sodomy with men and women. And the murders in Artaud's writing are usually gratifications of lust. The castration that results from an act of love will often be metaphorical, rather than literal: the act deprives the man of his chastity, and by implication it drains his creative energies. Preserving his chastity thus means, for the Artaudian male, safeguarding his resources.

Some critics link Artaud's sexually-bedevilled characters with their author. He was the first child in his family, sickly, and liable to have been spoilt. His mother seems to have doted on him to the point of possessiveness. He never married; his one engagement was broken off by his fiancée's father.[3] He had one sister. He probably felt what pop psychoanalysis calls inadequate vis-à-vis women, if only because of his fragile health. He had a Catholic upbringing. During his later years in asylums he underwent occasional delusions of being either Christ reborn or the Antichrist, the incarnation of purity of soul or the sink of all iniquity.

But we do not assume that because Sophocles retold the myth of Oedipus he was a latent parricide or had designs on his mother or abnormally feared castration. To suppose that Artaud shared certain traits with his characters is to confuse the difference between writing directly about one's life and feelings and plundering them for raw material in the invention of characters. The writer's equipment includes the peculiar under-standing and sympathy and ruthlessness that let his characters seem to speak for themselves.

But why did he settle on so many characters of such violence? Artaud drew on mythical stories. Myths commonly deal with conduct that is forbidden by such social constraints as norms, conventions and the law. Naming the forbidden, in prose or poetry, is a way of attempting to exorcise it, of admitting its temptations in order to release and dispel them. Enacting the forbidden in drama or social rites invokes the same desire to admit and dispel, except that it is more cleansing because actors, and to some extent spectators, simulate it, reproduce it, and in both senses of the term, play it out. Artaud worked veins of myth wherever he could find them.

Abnormal behaviour fascinated him. Not only did he write about exorbitant characters, he offered himself for exorbitant roles he heard about in forthcoming films and plays. His stated reason for doing this is worth noting. He felt that the anguish he had undergone qualified him for such parts. That is, he believed that brutality and other activities that exceed social norms proceed from anguish, although it does not follow, and

Artaud never hinted, that anguish must engender brutality. There is also, I would suggest, an unstated reason. The types of roles he went after are inherently dramatic. The character bears a terrific conflict within himself; he is not merely at odds with a sexual or any other kind of opponent. As a shrewd man of the theatre Artaud realized that such a character supplied both writer and actor with fat opportunities.

In his anguish Artaud was probably prey to more than the average share of forbidden thoughts and sensations. By immersing himself in forbidden material he may have hoped to practise on a personal scale something like the therapeutic exorcism he wished to carry out on a social scale. I hesitate over making flat statements about Artaud's personality. I do not believe one can scan an author's unconscious by taking his writing at face value and then deduce, as one critic does, that it was a 'fact' that he 'considered sexuality harmful, ugly, and sordid'.[4] Nor can I go along with another critic who says Artaud had an 'obsessive fear of woman and sexuality'.[5] His surviving letters to the actress Génica Athanasiou make it apparent that he loved her, and he had affectionate relationships with several other women. Jean-Louis Brau, who knew Artaud, has tackled the question of whether Artaud was a misogynist and mentions the many women with whom he was friendly and exchanged confidences. Brau concludes that he disliked, not women, but possessive women.[6] An unusually confessional author, Artaud puts a lot of himself into his writing, but what he takes out is something else. It is true that he deplores the division of mankind by gender,[7] but that too may belong to an artistic attitude, it may not have been a personal obsession. Artaud is hell-bent on bringing sexuality out into the light and freeing it from its romantic accretions. In the popular drama and in many classics (Goethe's *Egmont*, or Benjamin Constant's *Adolphe*, or the plays of Pierre de Marivaux) love was often an incorporeal yearning. It skirted what Artaud calls the 'forbidden zones' by declining to deal with the sexual act.

If the 'true theatre' is 'born out of a kind of organized anarchy', and if it 'frees the repressed unconscious, it is, among other things, a revolt and a liberation. Thus Artaud seemingly intends to strip sexuality of its sentimental disguises by going all the way. He will not fade out on a kiss or a clothed embrace but takes his audience into the very moment of orgasm, and then, in his anarchic fashion, denies them the satisfaction of a substitute release. Lovemaking, not merely 'love', becomes as controversial, discordant and upsetting as he can make it. It is one stage in the drama, not the last warm glow, one more station on the way to the catharsis.

The romantic vocabulary includes adjectives like magical, wonderful and mysterious. These are words Artaud took seriously. To restore their potency he had to subvert the older, mushier meanings that have descended from the ages of chivalry, when women were either workhorses or toys, and he then had to reimplant in these and other words a sense of the primitive, of the unrecovered.

CHAPTER 3: INSPIRATION AND ASPIRATIONS

1. On this matter of re-establishing order, see Bernard Beckerman, *Shakespeare at the Globe, 1599–1609* (New York: Collier, 1966), pp. 207–213.
2. There is even a conceptual unification present in Artaud's combative style of writing. He spends as much time, or more, stating what theatre is not as he does stating what it is and should be. Out of the encounter between the defensive, pathetic *is* and the glowing, summoning *ought*, he will contrive a theatre to exceed all others.
3. See Artaud's *Life and Writings*, p. 118. It is an open question whether or not Artaud's breakdown during his lecture in Brussels was an unconscious effort to stave off his approaching marriage to Cécile Schramme.
4. Bettina Knapp, *Antonin Artaud: Man of Vision*, p. 39.
5. Naomi Greene, *Antonin Artaud: Poet Without Words*, p. 128.
6. Jean-Louis Brau, *Antonin Artaud*, pp. 150 ff.
7. Many authors, Shaw and Strindberg among them, have envisaged the highest forms of humanity as being hermaphroditic.

II

History and Myth as Resources

4

From Antiquity On

Artaud's writings and his proposals, some of them never tested, touch those of many earlier artists, critics and other people, so closely that one can fall into the habit of referring to influences upon his work. But influence, a popular word in criticism, invites us to think that the later artist consciously imitated or borrowed from the earlier one when there may have been only a resemblance, a coincidence of interests, subject matter, or techniques.[1]

There is, for example, no evidence in his published material that he had read about the treatment of epilepsy and hysteria in Mycenean society, a millennium or more before the era of Greek tragedy in the fifth century BC. Yet his plan to induce by means of theatrical cruelty a state of violence in the spectator, and then to expel it, has much in common with ancient psychomedical practices that cast out a spirit or god believed to possess the epileptic or hysterical patient.

In a later period one secret society, the Corybantes, advancing the technique from medicine to magic, if not religion, initiated its members in a cleansing dance ritual that first aroused the candidates to an emotional fever pitch and then rid them of their temporary madness by purification. The two ritual instruments used were those associated with Dionysus, the flute and the drum. In conjunction with incantatory songs and dancing, they conveyed the initiates through an experience not dissimilar in kind to the one Artaud seems to have had in mind.

In primitive societies the expulsion of an indwelling spirit, whether a god or a demon, would be in the charge of a medicine man or exorcist who corresponds in many particulars to

Artaud's *metteur en scène*, that 'manager of magic'. As George Thomson points out, epilepsy and hysteria, originally regarded and treated in Greece as diseases, later became qualifications for 'a special class of initiates, consisting of persons who had a predisposition to some form of dementia'.[2] And just as an epileptic, subjected to the treatment of exorcism, was by the ritual metaphorically killed and reborn – transformed – in order to be purified, so the initiate for admission into the secret society was remade as a person by inducing and curing of a madness. Further, those 'persons who had a predisposition to some form of dementia' were looked on as having prophetic potential, the Greek words for madness, *mania*, and prophecy, *mantike*, being cognate.

In a disguised or modified form this ritual reappears in a number of Greek plays that feature an extraordinary character who falls into a spell of madness and is possessed not by a god but at the instance of a god or gods. Aeschylus's Orestes in *The Oresteia* is driven mad by the Erinnyes, or Furies, for having killed his mother. Sophocles's Ajax has insanity laid on him by Pallas Athene when he rampages among sheep and cattle in a pasture at night under the delusion that he is taking the lives of his fellow Greeks who have treated him unjustly. Euripides's Heracles goes berserk when, on the orders of one goddess, Hera, another goddess, Lyssa ('Madness'), makes him lose his reason and slaughter his wife and small children. Like Ajax, he believes that he is taking revenge on his tormentors, in this case the family of King Eurystheus who drove Heracles to perform his labours.

These three heroes share not only the experience of a bout of insanity but also an initiation into a new mode of existence. Orestes undergoes a promotion from outlawed matricide to heroic king once he has survived the attacks by the Erinnyes. Ajax and Heracles suffer a degrading from the heroic stature of supermen (Heracles is even a demigod) to ordinary men reminded of their mortality and of their powerlessness in the face of the gods. Heracles will subsequently go through a reverse initiation, death by burning, and win a place for himself as a fully-fledged god who is given the goddess Hebe as his partner. In all three instances, and in others, the mad episode seems to have been part of a myth before the playwright took it over and dramatized it. One is hard put to it to determine how much of the episodes we owe to myth and history and how much proceeds from the playwright's imagination. But certainly cathartic rites of initiation into the Orphic Mysteries, the Eleusinian Mysteries, the Pythagorean brotherhood, and other secret societies and fraternities are frequently alluded to in the fifth century and later, and they are relics of the older forms of initiation. Some of these Artaud knew about. He winds up his essay, 'The Alchemical Theatre', by speaking directly of the Orphic and Eleusinian Mysteries, their 'spiritual means of decanting and transfusing matter' and their 'projections and precipitations of conflicts, indescribable battles of principles'. Such conflicts of principle, between the hardships endured on earth by the body and the eventual deliverance of the soul, between the dire present and the celestial future, do appear to have been at the heart of the initiatory procedures.

But at least one significant change took place in the initiations of the Mysteries after the Mycenean era. The candidates were no longer people with hysterical or prophetic proclivities. The Orphic and Eleusinian Mysteries drew on ordinary people for their membership, many of them peasants and city workers. The Pythagoreans were exclusive, but according to rank and income, not by psychological selection. We might guess that the composition of the Pythagorean brotherhood was not much less democratic than that of medieval guilds or contemporary masonic lodges who welcome businessmen and solidly bourgeois citizens.

Aristotle's version of the catharsis, published in the *Poetics* and written or compiled late in the fourth century BC, probably between 335 and 322, comes something like a century after the flowering of the Greek drama. It marks another change in the ritual of initiation, for it is now deduced from the consequences of a tragic play. It applies not to candidates but to all spectators at a performance. It is the actors who take the role of initiating officers or surrogate priests, while the spectators become witnesses, rather than participants. Still, as Thomson reasons, the performances of Greek drama were very likely played at a high pitch of intensity and met with an openly emotional response, both the acting and its reception being far more abandoned than we are accustomed to in our own theatre. Each Greek spectator must have had a sense of being present at a ceremony for everybody and not a cool, almost objective entertainment. Furthermore, the performance at the Great Dionysia in Athens took place, at least in the formative years, during a celebratory season, early spring, and the festival lasted for less than a week.

Artaud's notion of a catharsis exceeds Aristotle's in that he wished to take theatre back to an earlier phase, a time when the members of the audience really were involved in the ceremony and had even more at stake than did the passionate but essentially passive playgoers of Aristotle's time. In addition, Aristotle was an observer, describing what he read, saw and heard.[3] Artaud was a performer, looking back into history for practices that would justify his new, old theatre to come. As a coincidence Artaud might have savoured, he finds himself alongside Aristotle on most drama bookshelves.

Nine tragedies by Seneca on Greek mythical themes and the disputed authorship of a tenth play, *Octavia*, have secured a place in textbook histories for the most prolific Roman writer after Cicero. Seneca's are the only specimens of Latin tragedy that have survived. But their standing among scholars is not high. They are said to be severe comedowns from the lofty works of Aeschylus, Sophocles and Euripides, full of 'fustian and bombast', goriness and unnecessary cruelty. Historians frown on Seneca's sententious language, his unintegrated choruses, and the absence of theatricality in his closet plays, which are assumed to have been composed for private readings rather than for performances. The sentiments he expresses in favour of the bucolic life and the desirability of shrugging off ambition and fame strike many people as being hypocritical in view of Seneca's own ambitious career as scientist, philosopher, statesman and diplomatic adviser to Claudius and Nero, although we have no incontrovertible evidence that Seneca the politician and Seneca the poet were the same man. At best, he is felt to have been a link between ancient Greece and the Elizabethan and Jacobean playwrights, who hugely admired him.

Artaud also admired him. While reading Seneca's plays he wrote to his friend Jean Paulhan, editor of the *Nouvelle Revue Française*, that the Roman poet knew 'better than Aeschylus' how to put into words the old mysteries of initiation; that Seneca 'seems to me the greatest tragedian of history'; and that his tragedies provided the finest '*written* example of what is meant by cruelty in the theatre'. In the plays Artaud felt 'the transparent effervescence of the forces of chaos' which 'groan under his words in the most sinister manner'.

It is true that Seneca dwells on the grisly aspects of the myths he chooses to retell. In his *Phaedra* a messenger describes the death of Hippolytus in gruesome detail; another messenger pays inordinate attention to the rending of flesh and the flow of blood in *Oedipus* when the king roots his eyes out of their sockets. In *Thyestes* a scene depicts Thyestes eating cooked portions of his own sons at a banquet concocted by his brother, and then trying to fit together the bits of body that are left after the meal. But if, like Artaud, we search for the positive qualities in Seneca and ask what he is doing with the tragic stories, rather than what he is failing to do; if we read the plays as independent works instead of taking the Greek plays as inevitable models, we find some extraordinary dramatic effects.

His Stoic determinism decrees that an evil act has its repercussions not only on the person who commits it and not only on the people he is close to and the society he lives in. The act runs through the entire universe like a colossal, uncontrollable plague. All of nature becomes implicated. There are earthquakes, storms, floods, tidal waves. Growing things are blighted and seared. For Seneca the Creation is a seamless entity; gods, man and matter are one, and all of them are affected – or better, *infected* – by the evil act.

In these plays, then, the stage, instead of being localized, becomes the whole universe, or the void. One of Seneca's favourite settings, especially for acts of magic or divination, is a dismal grove where the conjunction of the open landscape, shadows, obscurity, incantation, ceremony and violence terrify some of the characters (one of the commonest nouns encountered in Senecan drama is fear), and in an ideal performance would lay a similar spell of nervous fascination on the spectators. The Greek grove becomes Anywhere, an unspecified chamber of horrors, which a playhouse is peculiarly suited to embodying.

Artaud drafted one play called *The Torments of Tantalus*, which imitates Seneca's *Thyestes*. The draft has disappeared and we have no idea of how closely he hewed to the original myths of the house of Tantalus or to Seneca's version of them.[4] Even so, just as his conception of a catharsis is not unlike Aristotle's, so the mood of cosmic danger he wished to invoke compares with that of Senecan drama; it is plain in a number of his writings, especially in his short play *The Fountain of Blood*.

Early seventeenth-century playwrights such as George Chapman, John Webster, Cyril Tourneur, Thomas Middleton and John Ford, as well as Shakespeare, borrowed with acknowledgements from Seneca, whom they fervently studied. Their plays demonstrated the evils inherent in the manipulations of power, what was then called policy and today would be called expedience, political realism, or pragmatism,[5] and they followed Seneca in representing a wicked deed as a leak in the moral universe that had far-reaching and hideous consequences. To illustrate these consequences on a personal scale the playwrights devised scenes of depravity and mutilation. In *The Duchess of Malfi* Ferdinand offers his sister a severed hand; when Deflores in *The Changeling* cannot remove a ring from the finger of a man he has just killed, he cuts off the whole finger and presents it to his mistress. In *'Tis Pity She's a Whore* Giovanni stabs his sister while making love to her, and later flaunts her heart on the tip of his dagger; Vindice in *The Revenger's Tragedy* entices his enemy during a night sequence to kiss a skull's mouth opening which is smeared with poison.[6]

36

Such characters will go to any length to work revenge on somebody who has wronged them (or maybe not wronged them), to acquire position and wealth, or simply to defy society. Their wantonly barbarous acts suggest that they have caught some spiritual disease. Certain critics believe these characters personify their settings, the swarm of competing, intrigue-ridden principalities that added up to Renaissance Italy and Spain, as well as the Machiavellian court of France. The characters might be compared with blisters that appear on the skin of people struck by the plague, those outlets of the diseased body's corruption. They are blatant anti-heroes but, precisely on this account, the plays that contain them are inspired by a loathing of immorality. Artaud praised many of these oversized characters and their excesses, particularly the incestuous Giovanni in *'Tis Pity She's a Whore*, and hoped to stage some of the plays. No doubt he felt they provided as accurate a picture of modern, as of Renaissance, civilization.

In 1819, two centuries after the outburst of Jacobean tragedy, Shelley wrote *The Cenci*, which reads like a throwback to the seventeenth-century Jacobean versions of the Italian court settings and their Italianate intricacies of plotting.[7] It was this play that Artaud adapted for the sole production put on by his Theatre of Cruelty in 1935.

CHAPTER 4: FROM ANTIQUITY ON

1. A critic who likes to detect full-blooded influences has his work cut out for him by artists who quote a predecessor as having affected their art so that they can bathe in his glory.

2. In his invaluable book, *Aeschylus and Athens*, Professor Thomson devotes part of his last chapter, 'Pity and Fear', to a discussion of pre-Aristotelian rites that involve a catharsis of a sort. (New York: Grosset & Dunlap, Universal Library, 1966.) Here I am indebted to Professor Thomson's argument and one of his quoted sources, E. Fallaize and J. Hastings, *The Encyclopedia of Ethics and Religion* (Edinburgh: 1908–1918), Vol. 10.

3. For almost two millennia critics looked on Aristotle's treatise as

a rulebook, a sequence of dicta, rather than as notations for an analytical description.

4. The manuscript is referred to in a letter addressed to Jean-Louis Barrault, and a projected staging of the play in Marseille is discussed in several documents. (Artaud, *Collected Works*, Vol. 2, pp. 151–155.)

5. The modern or neo-Machiavellian brands of pragmatism, the art of the possible, or 'being realistic' in politics, would certainly have been disowned by those highly principled exponents of Pragmatism, William James and John Dewey.

6. Shakespeare's plays written in this vein of 'cruelty' include *Titus Andronicus*, *King Lear* and *Timon of Athens*.

7. Unlike the Jacobean authors, Shelley had lived in Italy and wrote *The Cenci* there; according to Mrs Shelley, he received 'the manuscript account' which 'a friend put into our hands . . .'

5

Into the Twentieth Century

It is possible to trace an astounding number of resemblances between Artaud's hoped-for Theatre of Cruelty and various arts of the nineteenth and twentieth centuries. In theatre alone we notice similarities to the chronicle form, to Symbolism, Surrealism, Expressionism, and the assorted staging techniques of a host of experimental directors. But Artaud was also a critic of painting, a film actor and scenarist, a translator of fiction, and a poet. His theatrical writings reflect his devotion to these other arts, and to music.

The modern era in the drama is generally understood to have begun in 1865 when Henrik Ibsen wrote *Brand*, and two years later, *Peer Gynt*. Modernity, however, has roots or preliminary outcroppings in the drama of two youthful German prodigies, Christian Dietrich Grabbe (1801–36) and Georg Büchner (1813–37). Their plays, like many later ones, use a chronicle structure. The narratives seem fractured, discontinuous. The basic dramatic unit consists of the scene, not the act. Between any two scenes there may be a hiatus, a conceptual gap or a large time break. The action then becomes a series of fleeting, contrasted tableaux which cover an extended period of stage time. Peer Gynt, for example, leaves home as a youth and returns as an old man. The chronicle form reminds us of the Elizabethan and Jacobean history play with its dozens of scenes, abrupt changes of setting, and lengthy time span. That form borrows its form from the religious, medieval play cycles. Büchner, Ibsen and especially August Strindberg appear to have consciously imitated the Elizabethan-Jacobean methods of constructing a play.

The chronicle, or epic, as it is more commonly known today,

allows the playwright a great deal more freedom than he would find in the conventional and constricting well-made play form. He can not only jump from one time to another one much later, he can reverse time or take scenes out of their natural sequence by putting in flashbacks or flashforwards. Ibsen, for instance, reveals more and more of his characters' past lives while the action of his play advances. That action expands simultaneously forward and backward in time.

This structural innovation, frequently drawn on in the past 130 years, is now a staple of filmmaking as well as playwriting. It gave birth to an even more broken form, the disguised narrative, the story that must be pieced together by the spectator. Certain critics to whom the story of many plays is not readily apparent have concluded that plays with a disguised story have no story.[1] In fact, practically every play has a story; certainly Artaud's do. Bertolt Brecht once wrote that there will always be stories just as there will always be new ways of recounting them.

There are even storylines of a sort in the one genre of playwriting that is often said to make do without them. The Surrealist plays of André Breton and his confrères were not conceived, only born. They came into being as a consequence of letting the pen or typewriter dictate to the brain by getting on to paper words or phrases that happened to emerge from the author's unconscious. Strindberg had attempted to write and paint without preconceptions in the 1890s and had called the process 'automatic art'. The Surrealists rediscovered the method in the 1920s and christened it, by coincidence, 'automatic writing'. Inspired not by Strindberg but by Alfred Jarry's Ubu plays (*Ubu Roi* [1896], and the later *Ubu Enchaîné* and *Ubu Cocu*) and by Guillaume Apollinaire's *The Breasts of Tiresias*, the Surrealist plays disintegrate accepted forms much more ruthlessly than the Epic does. They are artistically subversive, and it may well have been the rebelliousness of their authors, as much as the artistic techniques – sentences or single words and stage effects that do not obviously relate to one another – that drew Artaud into the Surrealist camp for a time and gave much of his subsequent writing a Surrealist colouring. He named his first theatre the Alfred Jarry, probably to tell the world that the theatrical insurrection started by Jarry was still bubbling.

Much as Artaud's plays, and staging devices, share with Epic and Surrealism a discontinuous structure that reveals stories by indirect means, so they share another characteristic with the plays grouped under the rubric of Symbolism. In the Symbolist drama of Stéphane Mallarmé and Maurice Maeterlinck the telling of a story takes second or third place to the evocation of the characters' prevailing states of mind, their moods in relation to the setting and to one another. All plays convey moods but in Symbolist works a fateful mood predominates. In murky groves not unlike Seneca's, in castle keeps, impersonal halls and other bleak interiors, the characters become prisoners of mysterious, even supernatural, forces. Maeterlinck's celebrated *Pelléas and Mélisande* presents a mood of lethargy and helplessness in the face of cruel destiny, broken momentarily by violent activity, a chase, a quarrel, or a murder. Two of the characters, the heroine Mélisande and an innocent child Yniold, seem to be in touch with spirit presences, other worlds. Mélisande herself might be a dryad or water sprite, an ancestress of Jean Giraudoux's Ondine. Yet the play moves forward relentlessly through its kaleidoscopic moods to a predestined and bitter resolution, the deaths of its three principals. Like Artaud, Maeterlinck admired the extravagance and fate-struck characters of Jacobean tragedy, and had translated *Macbeth* and *'Tis Pity She's a Whore* into French. Artaud, in turn, appreciated Maeterlinck, noting in the latter's writings 'certain thought patterns whose *relevance to the present day* is not remarked on enough', and also 'the unconscious fatalism of ancient drama' and 'an attempt to give life to forms and states of pure thought'.[2]

A drama of moods, when interpreted skilfully, should transmit to the spectators ineffable emotions of joy, fear and sorrow that can grow to states of intoxication at not being quite in control of oneself: ecstasy, tremulousness and profound sadness. Such feelings correspond to what Artaud sought to arouse in his audiences: a performance should take them 'out of themselves' while it works its magic on them, and then return them to reality still not entirely released from the spell.[3]

One of the English translators of Artaud's *Collected Works* claims that 'with Brecht he is the leading figure of European theatre in the twentieth century'.[4] Artaud and Bertolt Brecht do stand at opposing ends of the theatrical spectrum. Their theatres contrast so neatly and schematically that one can use either of them to reveal the shortcomings of the other. Yet Brecht and Artaud, dissimilar though they are in their ideals, content and style, share a contempt for the commercial theatre and both of them characterize it as intended for the stomach, rather than the intelligence or feelings: it is 'culinary' (Brecht); it is 'digestive' (Artaud).

The Theatre of Cruelty is no isolated phenomenon. In its ramifications it brushes against the contributions of many other modern playwrights, designers and directors. Richard Wagner dreamed of a total artwork, the *Gesamtkunstwerk*, in which music, scenery, legend and human performance would conspire to create an overwhelming theatrical experience. The Wagnerian opera and the Theatre of Cruelty have that overwhelming in common. Adolphe Appia prefigured Artaud in the deployment of light on stage. He applied a detailed lighting plan – at first to Wagner's operas, subsequently to plays – in order to bring inert sets into a plastic, or organic, relationship with the living performer. Vsevolod Meyerhold exploited the cubic volume of the acting area with the aid of 'constructivist' sets. Gordon Craig and Gaston Baty made their own attempts to subordinate the actor's and playwright's will to the director's.[5] The definition of the director's role had been expanded as a result of the efforts of Constantin Stanislavsky, Harley Granville-Barker, Otto Brahm and Terence Gray. Artaud benefited, directly or indirectly, from their pioneering efforts, and also from the advances due to scores of scenic designers in Europe, America and elsewhere in the first three decades of the century. Whether or not Artaud knew of the theories and work of these people, there are marked resemblances between their ideas and his.

Chapter 5: Into The Twentieth Century

1. The so-called 'new novels' of Butor, Sarraute, Simon and Robbe-Grillet are often cited as fiction that has no story or plot. But these novels do have stories, not always conventional ones, which become apparent when one studies the texts closely.

2. From Artaud's preface (1923) to Maeterlinck's *Twelve Songs*. (*Oeuvres Complètes*, Vol. I, 'Introduction', pp. 236–240.)

3. Artaud was strongly affected by the Gothic horrors in the supernatural fiction of Edgar Allan Poe and Matthew G. Lewis. He collaborated in translating Lewis's novel *The Monk*.

4. Victor Corti, *Collected Works*, Vol. I, 'Introduction,' p. 9. Corti's claim smacks of exaggeration. Artaud has had repercussive effects on world theatre – or this book would not have been written – but so have Shaw, Pirandello, Copeau, Beckett, and others.

5. Baty had protested about the tyranny of language (*Sire le mot*, 'his majesty the word') in theatre, much as Artaud had. He was one of the four members of the Cartel des Quatre, the others being Charles Dullin, Georges Pitoëff and Louis Jouvet.

6

Related Arts

We think of Artaud as being primarily a writer, but he was also attracted to the visual arts. Since his youth he had practised drawing, therapeutically during his stay in a Swiss hospital; later he produced many freehand sketches and portraits, most of them in pencil or pencil and wash. He sometimes analyses paintings for the cruelty of their content. In 'Metaphysics and the *Mise en scène*' he discusses Lucas van Leyden's *Lot and His Daughters*. In other places he refers approvingly to the art of Goya, Breughel, Bosch and El Greco. As a young personality-about-town in the 1920s he published brief reviews of gallery showings and exhibitions.[1] Toward the end of his life he wrote 'Van Gogh, Society's Suicide', a personal statement in which he reveals a feeling of kinship with that artist, his tortured life and visions.

Artaud's extant drawings and designs do not mark him as an unusually gifted artist but they make us aware of his consuming interest in the look of a stage, in creating the right environments for the action. He shows particular sensitivity in understanding how the play of lights, both the general lighting for illumination and the special spotlighting and colouring, a distinction first made by Appia, can rinse those environments in surprising emotional richness.

The silent films Artaud knew appear to have made multiple impressions on him. He observed the actors' movements, the scenic transitions (cutting and editing), light values and shadows, figure compositions, and the fluidity of viewpoint as the camera shifted position. Film directors clearly enjoyed far greater discretionary powers and opportunities than did their opposite numbers in the theatre. Artaud writes appreciatively of the movies of Chaplin, Buster Keaton, the Keystone Kops and the Marx Brothers. It is not merely the humour that wins him; he relishes their exploration of mime as an art form, and the subversive nature of their antics. The farcical eruptions of childhood pranks from Harpo, the cool insolence of Groucho, the balletic wonders of Chaplin, on or off his feet or skidding about on roller skates and banisters – these depict human movement taken to extremes that temporarily deplete the performer and outrage the other, normal characters.

On the face of it the statement that Artaud's theatre could incorporate the free-swinging, rebellious lunacy of film farce and the measured rhythms of the Balinese dance-theatre seems wilfully contradictory. But it also drew on the disciplined ritual he had observed, and taken part in, among the Tarahumara Indians during a visit to Mexico in 1935. Both the Balinese performance and the tribal ritual are formalized to the extent that one enactment is almost identical with any other: indeed, the beauty of both consists in their durability, in their having reached an accomplishment that does not need to be changed, much less improved. Yet the acting of Keaton or Chaplin is also measured and controlled with a precision that less conscientious artists do not attain. It is anything but the careless capering it looks like. We know that Fred Astaire's dancing patterns followed an intricately rehearsed plot; they fitted into a grid of numbered and lettered squares, so that the dancer's abandoned leaps actually took him to within fractions of an inch of where he meant to land. Much the same is true of Chaplin's scaling of a fence, Harpo's skirting of a statue as he rushes dangerously close to it in passing, or Keaton's near-tumbles over the edge of a waterfall. Once the frenzied act has been committed to film and been watched over and over, one can separate out the movements of hands and fingers, the head, the trunk, the legs and feet. The resolute preparation that made it possible becomes all the more evident. It acquires the qualities of ritual. One can almost hear behind it an insistent percussion like the ones that govern a Balinese dance or a primitive ceremony.

45

All in all, this considerable list of resemblances tells us that Artaud's work is, to take refuge in an overused word, eclectic. It unites a host of disparate effects, from the quasi-religious beginnings of theatre in the west to the tribal religious devotion that persists in other parts of the world.

CHAPTER 6: RELATED ARTS

1. Some of the reviews are reprinted in *Collected Works*, Vol. 2, under the heading 'Literature and the Plastic Arts'.

III

Artaud as Artist

7

Playwright

In the past century theatre has become a profession for specialists. We find people in the commercial arena who spend their working lives and sometimes erratic incomes as lighting designers, song arrangers, or writers of lyrics for musicals. Today any director needs multiple talents in order to urge the best work out of his specialized colleagues since he is finally responsible for the production's results. But the complete man or woman of the theatre is a rare specimen, the person who is actor, designer, director, critic and occasionally producer in one – who knows all the theatrical arts without necessarily functioning in all of them all the time. Even when we delve back farther into theatre history, Artaud has few predecessors in this respect. The three outstanding all-rounders are Zeami Motokiyo (1363–1444), who codified the principles and practices of the Noh theatre, and with his father, brought them to an exalted level of achievement; Jean-Baptiste (Poquelin) Molière (1622–1673), at first a founder and manager of L'Illustre Théâtre which toured France, but later the official provider in and around Paris of entertainments for Louis XIV; and Gordon Craig, Ellen Terry's son and a greatly respected actor during his twenties, who went on to devote himself to enlarging the scope of the stage director.[1] Like Artaud, Craig was a superb propagandist for theatre as an art, an idiosyncratic theoretician, and an artist who found fewer opportunities to practise than to preach.[2] Both men are known, then, principally for their repeated calls for a new theatre. The nature of that theatre-that-might-have-been is worth considering because, to some extent with Craig and emphatically with Artaud, criticism has restricted itself to doctrinaire assertions deduced from their manifesto-like summonses to action. But a summons is one thing, action another. The theories of an Artaudian theatre, even if they added up to one clear-cut doctrine, which they do not, would have gone through all sorts of modifications. The process of mounting a stage production consists of a series of revelations. The result, as it is presented to an audience, is unpredictable even if, like Max Reinhardt, the director starts out with an *Regiebuch* filled with specific notations of what is supposed to happen. One Artaud production would have been dissimilar to others, conditioned by the nature of the material, the personalities of the actors, the moods of the director, and other variables. In this section I will look at Artaud's artistry through three of his roles: playwright, actor and *metteur en scène*, and then raise a few questions and doubts about that artistry.

Not all of Artaud's plays have been recovered. The ones known to be missing are *Acid Stomach, or the Mad Mother*, directed by him at the Théâtre Alfred Jarry for two showings in 1927 and described as 'a musical sketch [the music composed by Maxine Jacob] . . . a lyrical piece, a comic exposition of the clash between theatre and the cinema',[3] and *The Torments of Tantalus*, completed in 1935, Artaud's presumed adaptation of a Seneca play. Since *Acid Stomach* was actually performed, its loss is all the more regrettable, especially if it had production notes to go with it. There may well be further works still missing. Artaud had the habit of jotting down summaries or 'scenarios' on odd pieces of paper like the backs of letters, hurrying them into prose notes, or dictating from them, as if to remind himself later of dramatic moments and images that had leaped out of his imagination. Other Artaud scenarios for the theatre exist.[4] They were published as extended stage directions and include *Paul the Birds, or The Place of Love*; *The Philosopher's Stone*, a mime with several lines of dialogue, written in 1931 and published posthumously in 1949; and another synopsis called *There Is No More Firmament*, probably written in 1931–32. *The Fountain of Blood*, a four-page drama published in 1925, belongs in the same collection (*Umbilicus of*

Limbo) as *Paul the Birds*. Only one full-length text for the theatre remains extant, that of *The Cenci* (1935), which is considerably shorter than Shelley's play of the same title.

Artaud can hardly have meant *Paul the Birds, or The Place of Love* to be enacted on a stage. Its two published versions differ from each other but both, written in prose with a few interspersed lines of speech, consist of descriptions of a dramatic situation, rather than developments of that situation.[5] As Artaud outlines it in the second version the play (if it is a play) does not grow or move; it takes place '*solely* in the mind' and seems intended as a sort of triptych: blurred portraits in one loose frame of Brunelleschi, Donatello and Uccello, the latter sharing traits with the author-painter, Artaud. Uccello is on 'one level', Brunelleschi and Donatello on 'another level' – whether higher or lower Artaud does not say – and on a 'little level' is Uccello's wife, Selvaggia, who does not take part but is referred to by the others. The mind in which the play exists is Artaud's, although he is trying by a terrific exertion of sympathy to make that mind work through Uccello's.

Looking out through a window on an evening exterior, Uccello debates with himself: shall he paint a portrait of his wife? She happens to be dying of starvation; perhaps he can capture her 'form', which is vanishing during these moments, 'beginning not to exist'. She is 'letting herself die for him' without reproaches. He thinks of her love for him and the absence of his love for her. She, as a compliant model, is an object to him, detached, unconnected. Brunelleschi, however, does love her, with a fierce, worldly, sensual love, and he chides her husband for allowing her to die. Uccello is, in a way, sensitive to Brunelleschi's accusations ('Yes, Brunelleschi . . . you are speaking in me'), but he cannot break out of his thoughts or refrain from manufacturing in his head a 'preconceived tirade on the place of art in the mind'. He has been, he realizes, a sculptor of 'nothing but the charnel house'. Trying to 'define falsehood in eternal time', he became a painter of corpses.

Here it is as though Artaud speaks simultaneously through

and to the mind of Uccello. The actual artist lived; he exists as a memory still; he also exists as a character dredged out of Artaud's recollections, what he remembers about Uccello and what he has seen of his work, and how he, Artaud, has responded to it. The Uccello of this weird work is both invented and a character who is conscious of himself as an invention.

Artaud suddenly breaks off the musings that are partly his, partly ones he attributes to Uccello, in order to write down a capsule description of the three male characters. Paolo Uccello, whose name translates into Paul the Birds, has a hardly audible voice and 'walks like an insect' (a simile which could mean almost anything); his robe is too big. Brunelleschi, an earthier, larger, more life-loving figure has 'a real stage voice' and 'looks like Dante'. Donatello is 'somewhere between' the other two; Artaud sees him as 'St Francis of Assisi before the Stigmata'. Selvaggia is not described. A last, separated portion of the work is a personal statement by Artaud telling of his being haunted by 'the theme of Paolo Uccello'. This haunting arises from the author's inability to concentrate his thoughts: 'I break down at every turn, my branchings off are legion.' He strives to find the right tone of voice, the fruitful theme, a firm intention, although the creating of art resists such certainties, and confronts the artist with one difficult choice after another.

The personal statement and the work end with what looks like certitude. The author, still speaking as himself, asserts that 'one can do anything in the mind', one can choose any tone of voice, any style, and change it at any time without ever being wrong or inept. In truth, this is a statement of regret, if not despair. Something 'spoken' in the mind, a confidence addressed to oneself, may need adjustments or even a transformation before it can become art, which is addressed to others. Artaud is saddened by his inability to transform into art the colloquy with his evocation of Uccello.

A number of images in the first version are omitted from the second. The two that appear most striking, most physical, are phallic. One image is Uccello's ripping out of his tongue, rendering himself speechless, and symbolically impotent, reducing his ideas to pure thoughts that cannot be uttered. The other image has to do with Brunelleschi, the most sensual of the three artist characters. He 'suddenly feels his tail swell up and grow enormous'. Out of it flies 'a great white bird, like sperm, which spirals as it turns in the air'. No explanation of such an image would be satisfactory, yet the reader has a sense of potency lost, wasted, escaped. The sperm-bird, like a child or a completed work of art, becomes its own master and has its own life. By omitting these two images in the second version of *Paul the Birds*, and by means of other editing, Artaud suppresses physicality and focuses on the mind. Much as his Uccello callously thinks of doing a portrait of Selvaggia, from whom the life is ebbing (soon she will be dead, sooner or later all his sitters will be dead), so Artaud attempts a 'mental drama' that deals with the bewildering, uncontrollable human mind in flux.

But why Uccello? One critic suggests that Artaud's Uccello resembles the original Florentine artist in being 'more interested in intellectual concepts than in living experiences', the evidence being the real Uccello's technical preoccupation with 'problems of perspective'.[6] But many artists have struggled with the formal intricacies of perspective: Uccello is no special case here. Nor does a concern with perspective have to preclude an interest in 'living experiences'. My own guess is that the name Uccello or *les Oiseaux*, 'the Birds', fascinated Artaud more than did the painter's life and techniques. It gave him a pretext for justifying the soarings of his own mind and their vertiginous falls in mid-flight. He casts himself as the character, yet remains partitioned off from the character. Assuming a role like this one, the role of a venerated artist, is a wishful act. I see no criticism of Uccello in the young Artaud's playlet, only a wish to be able to accomplish, to finish works of art. More brazenly than most dramatists, Artaud remakes himself as his hero, Uccello the thinker, flanked by Brunelleschi the doer, and Donatello the saint or 'be-er', whose life is exemplary. Thoughts, deeds, presence – these might almost be synonyms for the three artists as Artaud conceives them here, and his visions of them do not necessarily reproduce in any manner what they were historically.

Is it possible to create by thought alone? Where is 'the place of love in all this?' the play asks, echoing its subtitle. Love helps to nourish the artist. It 'gives him the impulse to create'. But such an impulse is only the beginning, the desire, the readiness for action; it is not part of this Uccello's process of creating. Once he has felt the impulse, he does not need love any more; he has taken and does not have to return it. He can see his wife dying, think about her in that condition, and paint her. He takes her love and gives back only his art. Let her die so long as she has served that art. Brunelleschi may yell at him for his callousness. He is not listening. Paul the Birds flies unhampered by the strings and burdens of giving love. Is such a figure enviable? Artaud is not sure. He is confusedly dealing with one of the questions posed by Ibsen in *When We Dead Awaken*: does an artist lack something as an artist when he fails to meet his obligations as a man?

It is often said that Artaud wishes to destroy dialogue, or at least to tame it and subordinate it to his theatrical business. This notion is refuted by two of his plays, *The Fountain of Blood* (*Le Jet de sang*) and *The Cenci*, in which the quantity of dialogue outweighs the quantity of stage directions. Spoken lines are not merely important in Artaud: because he is frugal with them they take on unusual significance. If he objects to conventional dialogue, what he dislikes in it is its conversational or argumentative tone. He wants his spoken material to be explosive in sound, equivocal in meaning, and unnatural in its delivery – that is, as theatrical as the physical activities – and he often specifies these requirements.

A short play that runs to only about five pages of text, *The Fountain of Blood* is not a scenario or outline, but a completed work. Artaud made subsequent revisions but they are minor ones. The play begins with a Boy and Girl who declare their love for each other and for the beauty and stability of the world, after which they flee out of sight to escape from a hurricane, a collision of stars, and one scorpion, one frog and one beetle that land on the stage to denote the plagues. Two older characters appear, an armoured Knight from the Middle Ages and a Wetnurse with oversized breasts. These two prove to be the parents of the Boy and Girl. The Knight eats Gruyère cheese and wants to look at his wife's breasts, but she goes offstage, troubled by the incestuous affair between her son and daughter.

The Boy reappears, saying he is looking for his wife. He meets a group of shadowy figures who represent, perhaps, different classes of society: a Priest, a Beadle, a Whore, a Judge, and others. The Priest tries to get the Boy to confess to some obscene sins, but the colloquy is interrupted by more gigantic disorders, including an earthquake, thunder, lightning and panic among the characters.

A huge hand reaches for the Whore and seizes her by her hair, which catches fire. The Whore retaliates by biting the adjoining big wrist. Thereupon, a 'fountain of blood' gushes across the stage, as though God's life, and most of the world's life, is being drained away. All the characters die, except for the Boy and the Whore. As if experiencing an orgasm, the Whore slumps into the Boy's arms.

The Wetnurse then returns with her breasts deflated and carrying the Girl, who is dead. The Knight asks for more Gruyère. In response, the Wetnurse lifts her skirt; she is showing him a 'hole' as a substitute for his hole-riddled cheese. This action terrifies the Boy and shocks the Knight.

Now we have a stage effect that calls for out-of-the ordinary theatrical means. Scorpions, a multiplication of the one that landed earlier, swarm out of the Wetnurse's clothing and over the Knight's sex, which swells, bursts and 'becomes glassy and glistening like a sun'.[7] The Boy and the Whore flee, 'like people trepanned'. The dead Girl ends the play when she revives, gets up and says, 'The virgin! Ah, that's what he was seeking.' This last baffling line could mean literally the Virgin Mary, or figuratively lost virginity or innocence, the Girl's or the Boy's own younger self.

The play amounts to a nightmarish, comic story in miniature of the creation of the world and its desecration by people, especially by women. It starts with the Boy and Girl in a state of bliss; when the Girl revives at the end it is as though a new cycle of creation is beginning.

55

The action contains two distinct elements. Side by side are a set of personal scenes written with dialogue, and a set of impersonal scenes, the cataclysmic happenings, expressed wholly in stage directions. In the personal scenes the Boy comes into contact with a triad of women and a triad of men. He is drawn to women and revolted by them. The Wetnurse-mother is his source of nourishment (milk, cheese); the Girl, of passion and inspiration (beauty, love, wonder); the Whore, of fleshly temptation. But the women are also the source of scorpions, infidelity and impurity, and they exhaust the fountain of life. The men stand for the Boy's dream of himself after the world corrupts him: as the Beadle, who is a cuckold; as the Knight, a father with only the vestiges and outward show of masculinity, the armour and the voyeurism, when he wants to look at his wife's breasts rather than to have her sexually; and as the Priest, a man with a calling and no faith. All in all, *The Fountain of Blood* is a tragic, repulsive, impassioned farce, a marvellous wellspring for speculation, and a unique contribution to the history of the drama.[8]

Unlike *The Fountain of Blood*, *The Philosopher's Stone* is a scenario by intention and would depend on a staging to fill out its conceptual and theatrical gaps. Artaud had such a staging in mind when he sent the script to Louis Jouvet in 1931, proposing it for a curtain raiser, a revolutionary contribution to Jouvet's conventional theatre. Jouvet, who was constantly in debt and managed to put himself temporarily in the black from time to time only by reviving his enormously popular performance of *Dr Knock*, was not impressed by Artaud's suggestion that doing revolutionary work was 'the only way to become commercial!!!' Even the exclamatory punctuation left him unmoved.

Artaud prepared the script for reading by putting in subheads, 'Decor', 'Characters', 'Summary' and 'Development', and by adding some explanatory production notes on voice and movement. The decor consists of a black frame, either inside or enveloping the proscenium arch. Within the frame and set at an angle to it, a red curtain hangs down like a backdrop and spills into folds on the floor. When opened in the middle it reveals an inner stage lit in red: this is the laboratory or operating theatre. A large table and a tall chair, the only properties, stand in the foreground.

The characters are Dr Pale, a surgeon reminiscent of the mad scientist of horror stories; his young wife Isabelle, full of sexual yearnings; and a visitor, none other than Harlequin from the Italian Comedy, who pretends to submit to one of the Doctor's fiendish experiments. These characters are given a few words, grunts and sundry other articulations, but they mime them; the actual sounds are voiced by an actor concealed in the wings so that one gets the impression that the characters are puppets.

In the first scene Dr Pale is hacking away at a pile of dummies and dismembering them. He tosses aside the stump of an arm and turns to Isabelle. She, 'imitating his movements like a distant echo' (another puppet effect), goes toward him and 'a long erotic labour begins', during which she 'shows a mixture of disgust and resignation' by clawing and otherwise hurting him while they make love.

A 'sort of period military march' introduces Harlequin, who enters with his back to the audience and announces that he has come to have the philosopher's stone taken out of him. Now, Dr Pale has been seeking the philosopher's stone, that wondrous dream of alchemists which was believed to have the property of transmuting base metals into gold or silver and of extending human life, perhaps indefinitely. He eagerly seizes Harlequin by the neck and propels him into the operating theatre, while Isabelle mimes an ecstatic dance and faints in rapture, but miraculously without falling.

Harlequin has two aspects. To the Doctor he presents himself as a bow-legged, one-eyed, crippled, trembling hunchback. But Isabelle sees in him a virile, chesty, young beau. The Doctor quickly discovers this second aspect, 'the real Harlequin', and brings him back on stage in order to chop off his legs, arms and head. Whether this little game is pure experiment, or part of the Doctor's search for the philosopher's stone (like the Boy's search for the virgin in *The Fountain of Blood*), or simply some enjoyable sadism we do not find out.

The Doctor's exertions finally tire him out and he falls asleep at the table, snoring noisily.

The trunk of Harlequin then retrieves its head, arms and legs in order to crawl over to Isabelle, who has come out of her faint and sits expectantly in the middle of the stage. There follows a 'violently erotic scene'. The lovers grasp each other's head, chest, stomach, shoulders and loins to demonstrate the depth and fervour of their emotions. They proceed to bounce into the air using each other's stomachs as trampolines. The Doctor cuts short their acrobatics by waking up. He advances on them threateningly. Disaster! But with astounding presence of mind Isabelle pulls a dummy replica of him from under her dress, a bright spotlight hits the infant, and the Doctor can only conclude that he, not Harlequin, is the father. He embraces Isabelle while Harlequin hides behind her. It is not clear which one of the trio is left holding the baby.

One could strain for some startling deductions by taking this playlet seriously.[9] I am inclined to see it as a farce. The situation comes right out of some Commedia dell'Arte scenarios about the cuckolded old husband; so do the names Harlequin, Isabelle and the Doctor (who was usually a pedant and a talky philosopher). Artaud has tricked out this old situation with a whiff of alchemy and some late Victoriana such as the red curtain, the melodramatic villainy of the Doctor and the 'period military march'. He evidently hoped that Jouvet, a knowledgeable man of the theatre, would appreciate this imaginative attempt to revolutionize a thoroughly traditional piece of material. But Jouvet gave him no encouragement. *The Philosopher's Stone* has been staged only posthumously.

The play *There Is No More Firmament* is Artaud's unfinished symphony. It consists of four movements, each complete in itself, with ample spoken lines and directions, and a heading, 'Movement V', with nothing to follow.[10] The composition is musical throughout, themes and variations in the dialogue and stage effects, with music employed more freely than in any of his other works. The form suits the material. This is an account of a natural (that is, unnatural) catastrophe, treated at greater length than are the ones in *The Fountain of Blood*. The catastrophe is recounted in language and images that remind one of some passages in 'The Theatre and the Plague', an essay written a year or two after the play and, very likely, its artistic by-product. Instead of individualized characters we find crowds, groups and choruses. The few people alluded to separately in the text have generic titles, not names: a Woman, a Policeman, the Doctor, the Inventor, and so on. This depersonalizing gives the impression that mere people are helpless before the onslaught of the catastrophe, during which the sky is 'physically abolished' and the Dog Star, Sirius, is located 'only a minute away' from Earth.

Movement I serves as a prelude, or, more accurately, an overture, in which the major and minor themes are sounded. An abstract opening calls for musical chords that 'are struck in the sky', and almost as if visible, pour to the ground, 'spread out in arcs', and pile up in layers. Next, colours flicker on and off in succession, starting with a red and ending in a faded, insipid yellow, 'the colour of dirty fog or the simoom' wind. The lights and music-with-sound then combine jaggedly and fade. Normal lighting prevails: we see a street intersection at dusk.[11] Over the medley of street noises and snippets of broken, everyday conversation, a 'haunting, monstrous voice' tries to make an announcement. The light and sounds die out 'as if a waterspout had sucked everything up into the sky'. A woman starts to undress; disconnected lines suggest the onset of a plague-like frenzy; men attack women and other men; a child wails; people feel as if they are on fire. Then the panic ends and life on the street returns to its normal pattern. It is a quiescent interlude. The first movement was only a foretaste of the disaster.

Movement II opens with scores of people crying out questions as they stare apprehensively into the sky. Do they see a celestial sign? The sun? The moon? Is something falling? They are supplanted on stage by news vendors with sheets declaring that there are no more Pyrenees and no more firmament.

Abolishing not just any mountain range, but the Pyrenees, in addition to the firmament, shows, if nothing else did, Artaud's genius for imagery. The Pyrenees, France's southernmost boundary, look on a map like a pedestal or base. To conceive of their disappearance is to imagine the country's geographical reality and stability menaced. The onlookers feel more and more bewildered by what they think they see and hear. Their disquiet is aggravated by a message from the government urging them to remain calm. Did something fall then? A comet? A thunderbolt? A mysterious disease? Some people feel cold, others as if they are on fire. A stretcher is carried past with a body on it. Another announcement: the sky has vanished; 'celestial telegraphy' and an 'interplanetary language' have been established to make contact, presumably, with Sirius. The crowd sighs with relief. It is another quiet moment, another lull before the storm. Arising out of the quiet we hear a revolutionary song.

Movement III ousts the middle-class world of the street and replaces it with the underworld: beggars, convicts, whores, cutthroats and pimps. The revolutionary song, counterpointed by the strains of the 'Internationale', brings on stage the underworld's most sick and deformed denizens, 'oozing on as if breathed up out of the lower depths', with their yellow and green, magnified, corpse-like faces, to make up a *tableau vivant* out of Breughel or Goya. A character called the Great Sniffer or the Great Pointer is borne into sight and dominates the proceedings. A grotesque figure with a tremendous snout like a dog's, he is the leader of the poor and the criminals, an overnosed Peachum or Dr Moriarty who smells the disintegration about him and determines that 'our time has come'. His followers jam themselves together and heave aloft banners, masts of ships, arched doorways and entire walls. They are ready to march, but Artaud is not ready yet to take the play all the way to its climax. Another brief interlude of quiet supervenes, the singing dissolves, the crowd files out and darkness returns.

Movement IV is distinctively satirical. A man called the Inventor paces on a platform built into a 'gigantic metal bridge' cantilevered out over the stage. The stage itself fills up with scientists and scholars who have the faces of bureaucrats. Some of them try to climb up to the Inventor's platform to question him. He descends (becomes accessible) and mimes replies which the other scientists criticize aloud ('You have done away with space . . . We are millions of light years distant from Sirius . . . This isn't science any longer; it's immoral'). The voices take on animal qualities: they sound like whistles, caws, baying, even the 'puffing of hippopotami in a cave'. The Inventor says that he is in touch with 'the forces' of Sirius. He is about to send out a signal to them when the curtain falls, a noise of air wells up, together with 'violent percussions', and the light turns cold. Then 'everything stops'.

Where would Artaud have taken the play from here? Doubtless he wanted to find a cataclysmic ending in the fifth movement that would top all that had happened in the preceding four. It is possible that his imagination ran dry or that he abandoned the project for want of encouragement, but my own conjecture is that he would have improvised the final movement in rehearsal, drawing further variations from his themes and perhaps adding a surprise. The movement might well have proved a conclusion to his earlier implication that man has tampered with forces beyond his knowledge, has tried to substitute himself for God, and will pay the price for his hubris and ignorance.

Yet the play's theoretical statements mean little when divorced from the theatrical means Artaud hoped to use and the strictly theatrical dividends they could bring. In this play, sometimes considered surrealistic, he has actually borrowed a great many formal devices from the Expressionists, who had been active in the second and third decades of the twentieth century. Indeed, *There Is No More Firmament* is the only out-and-out example I can recall of French Expressionism. Its massed characters with titles instead of names, its caricatures, its vehement rhetoric, its scathing of machinery and scientific discovery, its cinematic overlapping and cross-fading of scenes, and above all its portrait of modern civilization as a morass of insanity – these are all characteristics we associate with the turbulent writings of such Expressionists as Reinhard Sorge, Georg Kaiser and Ernst Toller. Yet the play is Artaudian

61

through and through: extravagant, authoritative and an open-ended quest.

Although never performed by Artaud, *The Conquest of Mexico* was intended for 'the first spectacle of the Theatre of Cruelty'. He therefore appends it to his essay, 'The Theatre and Cruelty (Second Manifesto)' in *The Theatre and Its Double*, as an exemplary text. At the beginning of the manifesto he announces that his theatre will devote itself to subjects and themes that correspond to 'the agitation and unrest characteristic of our epoch'. The operative word here is correspond, for the five-page *Conquest* dealing with Hernando Cortez's overrunning of Mexico and the Mexican peasantry, dramatizes parallels between historical Mexico and twentieth-century western life. It touches, Artaud hopes, on both historical and immediate issues that have to do with colonization and the Christian world's view of itself as innately superior to 'paganism and certain natural religions'.

As a spectacle the scenario is divided into four acts. The first, 'Warning Signs', creates 'a tableau of Mexico in anticipation' (anticipation of its rape by Spain) as it evokes an abstract portrait of the cities, ruins, caves and landscapes with the aid of lighting and music 'in the spirit of a secret lyricism ... overflowing with whispers and suggestions'. The actual 'warning signs', like the comparable effects in *No More Firmament*, presage a storm: shadows and light pieces of material 'pass through the air like distant meteors'. The act flows into a mime of Montezuma gathering with his priests and set off by a representation of the signs of the zodiac. As a counterpoint, a threatening image is seen of Cortez, his men and his 'tiny battered ships', which have crossed the ocean.

The second act depicts Mexico as Cortez the plunderer contemplates it: a mysterious terrain of silence, immobility, magic, 'cities like ramparts of light, palaces on canals of stagnant water'. A 'heavy melody' suddenly gives way to a single piercing note, like a scream. 'Heads crown the walls', reads a cryptic instruction, probably intending that masks of suffering are raised behind the wall on poles, like a multiple apparition. The battle is joined in the final scene of this act as Montezuma walks deliberately toward Cortez. The title of this act, 'Confessions', presumably tells us of Cortez's misgivings and unease, not exactly pangs of conscience or regrets, more like his sense of being a bull in a china shop appalled by the fragility of these strange surroundings.

The third act, 'Convulsions', opens with tableaux of revolt 'at every level of the country' and 'every level of Montezuma's consciousness'. The magical aura of Montezuma – his double role as political and religious leader – is expressed in divided appearances: several actors are to play him at once, differently lit and dressed. While battles are enacted on stage stylistically, we see the Mexican and Spanish leaders disputing with their advisers while the people sneer at them. The 'rebellion breaks out'. Artaud must mean here that Mexico has already been subdued and the people have risen against the invaders without our actually witnessing the acts of conquest. 'Convulsions' closes on a frenzy of fighting: gestures, faces, eyes, breast-plates, horses' manes, some of them seen as projections or paintings – an explosion of ritualized carnage.

The last act, 'Abdication', adverts to the later consequences of the invasion after Montezuma dies and the revolt is crushed. Cortez and his men argue over treasure. Nobody really controls the country. A band of Indians massacre a band of Spaniards. Diseases spread, 'poisonous blooms burst close to the ground'. This is the time of plague and the curious lusts it engenders. For the first time we see a woman's head. The funeral rites of Montezuma are conducted in an atmosphere of rotting and sickness with 'immense Spaniards on crutches'. Some of them will be cornered by the Mexicans and 'squashed like blood'. The conquest of Mexico has destroyed the conquerors, as well as the country.

As in all his plays Artaud would have required a large stage sufficiently equipped to allow for simultaneous playing of several scenes: the massed bodies, fighting and riots, mirrors in the corners of the stage to give the illusion of glittering treasure, and the simple moments of individual figures isolated in their indecision, selfishness, or panic – an emaciated peasant gorging soup, one or the other leader, a wounded soldier. The technique Artaud borrows in jumping from image to image is noticeably akin in this scenario to cinematic montage. As in the greatest editing sequences in film, the effect of rapid juxtapositions in time would build to effects on a spectator that are not quite analysable but propel him through spasms of thrilled wonder.

Yet the overall impression is anything but vague. No romantic sentiments are permitted to interfere with or undercut the concentrated brutality of *The Conquest of Mexico*, as happens in say, Peter Shaffer's *The Royal Hunt of the Sun*, or earlier dramatic versions of Spain's incursions into the American continents, such as Guilbert de Pixérécourt's *Pizarro* or August von Kotzebue's *The Spaniards in Peru*. Artaud gives us an imperialism with no redeeming, humanized qualities.

In his last work for the theatre, a fully wrought script, not a scenario, Artaud wrote a domestic-political drama but set it during the Renaissance. It follows pretty closely the lines of Shelley's *The Cenci*, even matching it scene by scene most of the way through in the plotting; that is, the disposition of characters in relation to one another on stage, but in severely condensed form.[12] Shelley had been inspired by a manuscript

communicated to me during my travels in Italy, which was copied from the archives of the Cenci Palace at Rome, and contains a detailed account of the horrors which ended in the extinction of one of the noblest and richest families of that city during the Pontificate of Clement VIII, in the year 1599. The story is, that an old man having spent his life in debauchery and wickedness, conceived at length an implacable hatred towards his children; which showed itself towards one daughter under the form of an incestuous passion, aggravated by every circumstance of cruelty and violence. This daughter, after long and vain attempts to escape from what she considered a perpetual contamination of body and mind, at length plotted with her mother-in-law and brother to murder their common tyrant. The young maiden, who was urged to this tremendous deed by an impulse which overpowered its horror, was evidently a most gentle and amiable being, a creature formed to adorn and be admired, and thus violently thwarted from her nature by the necessity of circumstance and opinion. The deed was quickly discovered, and, in spite of the most earnest prayers made to the Pope by the highest persons in Rome, the criminals were put to death. The old man had during his life repeatedly bought his pardon from the Pope for capital crimes of the most enormous and unspeakable kind, at the price of a hundred thousand crowns; the death therefore of his victims can scarcely be accounted for by the love of justice. The Pope, among other motives for severity, probably felt that whoever killed the Count Cenci deprived his treasury of a certain and copious source of revenue . . . (Preface to *The Cenci*, 1819).

I lift this generous quote out of Shelley's preface, not only because it superbly summarizes his tragedy, but because the three principals, and their motives as he enunciates them, are picked up faithfully by Artaud. Cenci's monstrousness figures in Artaud's opening scene and generates the play from then on. Beatrice's corrupted innocence, the main antagonistic force, becomes the theme of his final scene and is reiterated in the closing line, and Clement VIII's greed brings about the play's resolution. Artaud's Pope, like Shelley's, is not a character in the play, only a power in the background, but Artaud goes further than Shelley. He tells us, through a papal legate, that Clement did not merely feel that the Cencis had 'deprived his treasury of a certain and copious source of revenue', he unabashedly makes away with the entire family so that the Vatican will take over the Cenci inheritance.

In his Count Cenci Artaud contrived a portrait of unredeemed evil, a man with no glimmering of conscience, who blames God or fate for having made him what he is. His motto, like Andrew Undershaft's in *Major Barbara*, might well be 'Unashamed'. The play begins with a colloquy between him and Cardinal Camillo, in which we learn that Cenci has committed another murder. The Pope, says Camillo, will wink at 'one body more or less' provided that Cenci hands over about a third of his estate. Cenci replies that this demand gives him an excuse for making war on the papacy; he will certainly not surrender his property, nor does he wish to 'bury' his crimes. He is proud of them, he means to indulge in more of them, they will be more 'exquisitely refined' than ever. To excel in crime in his 'destiny'.

From then on the Pope is Cenci's enemy. Through Camillo and a prelate, Orsino, who courts Beatrice, the members of the family are encouraged to assassinate the old man. But Cenci himself plunges deeper into his career of crime and defiance. In front of guests at a banquet he gloats that two of his sons have been killed, possibly with his connivance, he drinks wine as though swallowing, and revelling in the taste of, their blood, and he threatens the assembled guests with death. He goes on to accuse the rest of his family of concocting plots against him, and decides to escort them to a castle where they will be imprisoned. He rapes his daughter, Beatrice, who infatuates him.

Beatrice, together with her ailing younger brother and her stepmother, a mild young lady named Lucretia who is Cenci's second wife, make up their minds to escape from their oppression by killing Cenci. So does another brother whom Cenci has disinherited. The old man escapes being murdered once, but the second time, at Beatrice's urging, two hired thugs stab him and drive a nail into his head. The assassins are selected because they are both mutes, but when the killing is discovered their muteness offers no protection. They are tortured until they confess in writing.

The last scene of the play presents Beatrice in jail, attached by her hair to a wheel, awaiting execution. The Pope wants her to sign a confession; he has already determined, without the aid of a trial, that she is guilty. Before she goes out to her death in a procession, 'a sort of pre-execution march' that sets off to 'the sound of an Inca seven-part rhythm', Beatrice confirms that her father did succeed in leaving a 'legacy of horror' when she says, 'Death may teach me that I have ended by resembling him.'

The action of *The Cenci* is by no means straightforward as this précis implies, nor, as we would expect in Artaud, does the dialogue do all the work. The scenic effects make a contribution that enriches the play's implications, much as they do in Seneca and the Elizabethan drama. Thus, Scene One takes place in a 'deep, winding gallery'. The sequence during which the mute assassins make their first attempt on the Count's life is accompanied by a storm and a violent wind that force the actors to move unnaturally and to shout, rather than talk. 'We ourselves are the hurricane,' Camillo says, 'so scream your lungs out if you wish.' The sounds of the words even become detached at times from the action, like autonomous presences, as when seven or eight people cry out Cenci's name, and 'then the voices grow louder and pass by like a flight of birds very close at hand'. (Such words, we can assume, would be intoned into microphones or megaphones by offstage speakers.) When Beatrice is being tortured, it is the wheels and beams of her jail, not she herself, that scream, grind and moan. And at Cenci's banquet, among the guests played by living actors there are dummies, looking like inhuman reproaches. Artaud says in an introduction that the dialogue will 'act as a reagent' to the other elements, the rhythmic gestures and movement, the play of the lighting, the colours of the sets and costumes, and the bursts of music.

The speeches themselves, extremely formal, almost incantatory, have a measured, even stilted precision that has nothing in common with the spontaneous conversation prevalent in plays of the 1930s. They conform to a predominantly French tradition that extends from Corneille and Racine to Jean-Paul Sartre, Jean Giraudoux and Samuel Beckett, a tradition of writing in generalized statements about life, or about a life, that have a paradoxical cast to them: 'Evil must be granted its portion of pleasure' or 'Popes are created by the exercise of cynicism' or 'I am rich but I have not yet profited from the possessions that a life of deceit seemed to place within my reach.' At times the dialogue falls into stichomythia, those exchanges in which words are echoed by successive speakers:

LUCRETIA: My God!
CENCI: Devil take your God.

LUCRETIA : But with such words no society can survive.

CENCI: The family which I have created and which I command is my sole society.

LUCRETIA: This is tyranny.

CENCI: Tyranny is my one last weapon to frustrate the war you are plotting against me.

LUCRETIA: There is no war, Cenci, except the war raging in your head.

CENCI: There is the war you are waging against me and which I am more than capable of returning in kind . . .

(Act II, Scene 1).

These scenic and verbal artifices remove the play from psychological literalism. They help to present Cenci's lust for his daughter, say, as an aspect of his lust to commit crimes, to uncover himself to himself through criminality. The incestuous act is a form of self-love, and a further step in his ambition to destroy what the Pope's man calls 'the social façade'. Cenci delights in progressing from the antisocial gesture to the unnatural one, as part of his quest for himself. In so characterizing him, Artaud consciously imitates the immorality of fate in the Greek drama. Cenci exclaims: 'Let those who condemn my crime first indict fate.' Beatrice later entertains the same idea when she reflects that 'neither God nor man nor any of the forces that dominate what is called our destiny have chosen between good and evil'. According to Artaud, the gods of Greek antiquity were 'oblivious of the pettifogging human distinctions between good and evil, almost as though they equated evil with betraying one's nature, and good with remaining faithful to it, whatever the moral consequences. Indeed, the gods never concerned themselves with moral consequences.'[13] While expressing no admiration for Cenci's personality, Artaud nevertheless appears to have admired his eagerness to defy social and moral convention and so become a first-rate candidate for enshrinement in a drama. Like Artaud's other plays, *The Cenci* is not quite a warning. It allows glimpses of its author's envy for a superhuman creature of fiction who resembles Molière's Don Juan in his delight at breaking the rules.

As a whole the play, according to a letter Artaud wrote to André Gide several months before the opening, attacked the 'antique notions' of society, religion, justice, order, and the coherent, unitary family. Still, it was not, Artaud cautioned, 'pure anarchy', for, while inveighing against the idea of order, an artist like himself might well have some personal respect for people who practised order, just as he might want to dispense with the idea of family ties and yet feel inevitable affection for his own family.

Chapter 7: Playwright

1. Craig was not a playwright, as were Zeami, Molière and Artaud, in that he did not compose dialogue. But he believed in imposing his own stage directions on play texts, and even considered the playwright who wrote in such directions to be a trespasser on the stage director's territory.

2. Craig's ideal theatre, envisaged from his essays, letters, drawings, and the magazine he edited, *The Mask*, appears a great deal cooler and more restrained than Artaud's does. If Craig is a mountain, Artaud is a volcano. Further, Craig's autocratic temperament made him less of a working partner for the actors and designer and technical staff than Artaud was.

3. *Collected Works*, Vol. 2, p. 33, and p. 217, note 18.

4. Artaud also left a number of film scenarios; one finished film, *The Shell and the Clergyman*, was based on his screenplay. A radio play called *To Put an End to God's Judgment* was recorded but not broadcast in Artaud's lifetime. These non-theatrical writings will not be discussed here.

5. The two versions are translated in the *Collected Works*, Vol. 1, pp. 51–54 and 147–151. The first volume of the French revised and corrected edition includes a footnote that refers to an untraced third draft.

6. Bettina Knapp, *Antonin Artaud: Man of Vision*, p. 30.

7. Some translations have it that the scorpions swarm over the Wetnurse's sex, rather than the Knight's (the French words *son sexe* being ambiguous). But the swelling, bursting and the sun

image seem to me more plausibly a reference to the male organ of the Knight. In addition, the scene suggests not only that the Wetnurse is 'infected' with scorpions but also that she transmits the infection to the male species.

8. The discussion here of *The Fountain of Blood* is a summary of the lengthier and more detailed study included in *Contradictory Characters* by Albert Bermel (Second Edition, 1996, Evanston, Il.), pp. 256–268.

9. Bettina Knapp (*Antonin Artaud: Man of Vision*) takes it very seriously indeed, seeing in it the story of Artaud's 'enormous struggle and preoccupation with his health' and 'new light shed on Artaud's inner development', loads of 'symbolism of the most basic kind' analagous to Wagner's four operas of *The Ring of the Niebelung*; a quest by the author for his identity; Isabelle as a representation of 'too much sexuality' and Dr Pale as 'too much intellectuality' – Artaud suddenly becomes a salesman for the golden mean – and a spirituality (the bouncing up and down of Harlequin and Isabelle) that 'implies a total negation of the physical world'. To Ms Knapp's credit she does attempt to say something about this and other plays, whereas some critics glance off each of the plays with an evasive sentence or two.

10. Two versions of the play, in handwriting and typescript respectively, have a number of differences in the detail, mostly the result of editing, but the changes do not substantially alter the play's meanings or form.

11. In some notes written on the back of the manuscript copy, Artaud seems to imply that this play might be performed in the street, police and weather permitting, if he could not come by a playhouse. It is safe to say that this is an afterthought. The production as Artaud envisages it requires a sophisticated light board and independently mounted spots, besides complicated acoustical arrangements and an elaborate decor.

12. Artaud claims that his play was based on (*d'après*) the work of both Shelley and Stendhal, but Stendhal's manuscript is little more than a translation – a most elegant one – of Shelley into French.

In a letter to Louis Jouvet Artaud 'insists', however, that his *Cenci* is an original, modern tragedy. He took from Shelley, he says elsewhere, only the subject matter, and for Shelley's 'lyricism' he substituted 'action'. This is not true except insofar as the Artaud play is much shorter than Shelley's.

13. From an article published in *Le Figaro* shortly before opening night, and reprinted in the English edition of *The Cenci*, translated by Simon Watson Taylor (New York: Grove Press, 1970).

While it is true that the gods in Greek drama are 'immoral' by Christian standards of good, evil and justice, one can detect a kind of morality, or at least a religious consistency, underlying their behaviour and commands that is persuasively proposed and defended in Anne Burnett's book on Euripides, *Catastrophe Survived* (New York: Oxford University Press, 1971).

8

Actor and Director

Artaud received his training and his early stage roles from Charles Dullin, one of France's leading directors in the generation after Copeau. He was entrusted by Dullin with a variety of parts, the most considerable of them being that of Basilio, the Polish king in Calderón's *Life is a Dream*.[1] Other actors who worked with or for him were struck by his boldness, his unorthodoxy of gesture and facial expressiveness and voice, the vividness and agony of the inner visions he deemed it necessary to draw on in order to give outward play to a character's feelings. He meant to be memorable. Where another actor would walk across a stage, Artaud might crawl, hop, or limp, to give every pace his studied, concentrated all. He put little stock in casualness or expertise, both of which implied for him a performance any other actor could manage. He sought for essences; these were what he came to admire in the oriental theatre, and what he later wrote about in his essay, 'An Affective Athleticism', which mentions the key centres in the human body 'on which to base the soul's athleticism'. There are, he remarked, '380 points in Chinese acupuncture, with 73 principal ones, but many fewer crude outlets for human affectivity.' In this essay he writes about learning to breathe, doing strenuous exercises, not only for taking in breaths, but for emitting them, so as to manifest 'the soul's desperate claims'.[2] Although the essay is a postlude to most of Artaud's acting career, it testifies to the intensity of his previous work in the theatre. What had probably begun as a desperate effort to speak through his body about his physical and mental suffering grew into a formulation of the need to expel that suffering by sublimating means. Artaud would not, then, have apologized for acting out of personal necessity. If acting is a creative, not merely an interpretative, art, as he believed, the anguish would enhance the actor's precious individuality.

One would expect from his writings and his unwillingness to spare himself that, as a director, Artaud would be a taskmaster. According to Raymond Rouleau and Tania Balachova, who played in his production of *A Dream Play*, the opposite was the case. Their rehearsals with him provided a release in the evening after they had spent a gruelling day working with Dullin or someone else. Artaud encouraged them to test out new voices, expressions, movements, to free themselves from old habits and routines, and achieve an unprecedented freedom in their acting. Their discoveries would presumably stimulate his own. He did not come to rehearsals with plans or hard-and-fast ideas, but operated out of introspection and intuition. Rouleau remembered that 'he seemed to listen attentively to the promptings of his unconscious'. Artaud might supply the actors with hints or suggestions but he did not insist that his way was the right one, nor did he specify what he wanted. If he demonstrated a reading of lines or an emotional state for the actors, it was to incite them to unleash their own imagination. Rouleau recollects that

> at the first rehearsal, Artaud rolled around on the stage, assumed a falsetto voice, contorted himself, howled, and fought against logic, order, and the 'well-made' approach. He forbade anyone to pay too close attention to the 'story' at the expense of its spiritual significance. He sought desperately to translate the 'truth' of the text, and not the words. It was only after he felt that he had found the truth, which his interior voyage had disclosed to him, that he fixed it meticulously, often with amazing profundity.

Rouleau adds that this antiliteral approach to acting could result in a performance in which the actor 'might begin a speech while standing up, but as he continued to speak he would fall to his knees, then lie down on the stage, and finally finish the speech on his knees. The audience thought the actors were ridiculing them.' Rouleau, who became a prominent theatre and film director, and acknowledges a debt to Artaud, observed that he had 'seen nothing since then to equal or approach his method, except perhaps the one that Tania Balachova, who was one of his disciples, uses in her dramatic art courses'.

Mme Balachova recalls that *A Dream Play*, in which she had the enormous part of Indra's Daughter, used an almost bare stage, beautiful, elaborate costumes, an unusual quantity of white colouring in the make-up (the pallor of fragile human beings or the pallor of clowns?), a few objects 'in very strange places – it was pop-art in embryo' – and 'no histrionics or declamation'. As in much Surrealist theatre, the objects evidently acquired something like personalities. The actors looked upon the performance as an 'adventure'.[3] It is remarkable how often the word adventure crops up in discussions of any aspect of Artaud's theatre. The same is true of the word magic. Benjamin Crémieux, an important French critic and translator of Luigi Pirandello, among other playwrights, reviewed *A Dream Play* and concluded that Artaud's art was 'a matter of rediscovering magic, of poetry in the everyday world, of bringing to light new relationships between human beings and things'.[4] Through acting Artaud was striving to bring the body's living presence into a natural harmony (natural for the stage) with its inanimate surroundings and with those 'forces' that impinged on it from within and without.

Artaud had hoped to follow his production of *The Cenci* with his treatments of *The Conquest of Mexico*, *Macbeth* and *The Torments of Tantalus*, the latter being a projected reinterpretation of the myths of Tantalus and the two sons, Thyestes and Atreus, who vied for his crown. *The Cenci*, which was not itself the true Theatre of Cruelty, would pave the way for these other spectacles by impressing audiences and potential backers, so that he would henceforth have a community of supporters to rely on. *The Cenci* did not win him such supporters. Some of the subsequent reviews were kindly, surprisingly so when one considers the drastic innovations Artaud was putting before critics, most of whom wanted nothing better than to go on contending with boulevard offerings. Nor was the reception irate enough to let Artaud parlay his work into a *succès de scandale* or to depict himself as a reborn Victor Hugo trying to introduce another *Hernani*.

The Cenci is thus, strictly speaking, a forerunner of the Theatre of Cruelty that should have materialized but never did. It was Artaud's last production and his one theatricalization of which we have much of a record.[5] The description that follows must be read as what Artaud actually achieved in the theatre, not what he meant to achieve, and as impressions of how his play looked, sounded, and was undergone as live theatre. He said he had taken from Shelley only 'the subject matter' and had wrought that material in such a way as to 'replace [Shelley's] lyricism with action', action being 'the true language' of theatre. The claim is not quite fair, for some of Shelley's lines are interpolated into Artaud's script, the scene-sequence of which, with a few exceptions, also follows Shelley's pattern. However, Artaud means to stress his intentions of keeping all the component parts of his production active and contributory, and of reducing the significance of the text in relation to the other components.

The production, a noisily heralded event, opened 6 May 1935, at the Folies-Wagram Theatre, a house that usually accommodated straightforward boulevard plays. The sets, designed by Balthus, were dominated by a partly realistic, partly abstract version of the Cenci castle with lofty ladders, columns, nets and irregular scaffolding behind it. Italianate stairways, arches and balustrades created an ambiance at once indoor and outdoor, rather like a comment on the magnificent stairscapes wrought by those greatest of Baroque designers, the Galli da Bibbiena family. But the arches were chopped off in the middle to enhance the depth and height of the stage space, and small painted curtains descended for the scene changes (such as the final one which carries the play from the castle to a torture dungeon), without obscuring the background.

75

Artaud told an interviewer that the sets 'were conceived in a spirit of true grandeur and are made only of real elements'. He also spoke of the symbolism of the costume colours, such as 'green for death, yellow for evil death'. The costumes themselves, also the work of Balthus, dressed the female characters mostly in two-piece gowns with puffed shoulders, full-length skirts, modestly ruffed necks and cinched waistbelts. The men wore doublets and tights, the former having the outlines of the ribcage, pectorals and the arm musculature stitched on, as though to project outward the structure of the body. In revealing internal features summarily on the surface, the costumes were therefore at one with the castle setting. Most of the men wore cloaks thrown back and flat velvet caps. As Cenci, Artaud was garbed in black with light-coloured stitching and ruff, so that he stood out in contrast to the other characters, especially to Beatrice. I would surmise that there was no accident in the resemblance between his costume and the traditional appearance of Hamlet. One critic observed that Balthus had 'dressed the contemporaries of Henri IV as the contemporaries of Louis XII', but it is unlikely that Artaud desired historical veracity, only a generalized historical tone. There are no coloured photographs of the production but the chosen colours seem to have been anything but vivacious and pleasing; they were either sombre or gaudy and troubling.

Another visual element, the movement, was also theatrically nonconformist. Artaud wished to formalize it, bring it closer to dance, and do away with a natural, unselfconscious gait. According to Roger Blin, who played one of the assassins, he wanted the princes in the banquet scene to imitate animals by bounding or gliding about. The actors struck poses or grouped themselves artificially; each pose, like each gesture, was to transmit and summarize a state of feeling. A note written on the playscript by Artaud even mentions an 'identification between a state of the world and the anger of old Cenci', a reminder of that seamless universe postulated in Seneca's plays, wherein men, moods and things are a single creation.

Some diagrammatic sketches in crayon reveal how Artaud mapped out his open floor space (he used few properties) by tracing the actors' relative movements: where they would meet, separate, cross paths, circle one another and take up individual stances. Such planning would today be considered mechanical, if not authoritarian, by actors and directors, but it may be that the diagrams were only a starting point and that the actors could later bring their own initiative to bear. Earlier, I have quoted Raymond Rouleau's remarks about Artaud's preference for improvisation seven years before during the rehearsals at the Théâtre Alfred Jarry. Possibly his directing approach had hardened. He was desperate for *The Cenci* to succeed according to his lights, sensing that he would not have another opportunity to prove himself. Or he may have wanted to take as few chances as he could during a limited number of rehearsals and with a number of inexperienced actors. He said before the opening, 'I do not believe in a professional career, and loathe everything this word stands for [the word professional], but I do believe in temperament and work . . . Professional actors who have kept themselves "pure" are rare.'

The audible components of the production included sound effects and music, as well as speech. Artaud worked especially hard to make the actors' voices more versatile. He wanted the spoken text to acquire a varied theatricality, instead of becoming a recital of information and feelings. It must be intoned, shouted, whispered, wheezed, howled and groaned, sometimes in contradiction to the denotative meanings of words and sentences. He compiled a complete voice scenario, but the actors had trouble following his instructions, and by the first night Artaud himself was hoarse, whether because of his demonstrations of how to croak and scream or because of the vocal strain of running rehearsals. Some of the lines were almost sung, for example, an incantatory lament by Beatrice. This is a throwback to the Greek theatre.

The reviewers, desensitized by countless snortings-out of the classics to the instrumental variations the human voice is capable of, attacked this aspect of the production most severely, some complaining because they had not been able to hear what was being said, others relieved for the same reason, yet others advising Artaud that, in producing a tragedy, he should look to reproduce tragic sounds – that is, to do things the old way.

If the actors had difficulty making their voices heard, that difficulty must have been compounded by competition with the sound effects of recorded footsteps and rhythmic stamping, stormy winds and waves accompanied by lightning flashes, the ticking of a metronome, the clacking together of wooden blocks, notes from a Martenot organ, the recorded chimes of Amiens Cathedral relayed through four distributed loudspeakers (to give the first stereophonic sound in the theatre), and the recorded humming-whirring of a factory for the torture scene. There were, in addition, interjections of pre-electronic but atonal music composed by Roger Désormière, ending in a seven-part Inca rhythm. Such sound and music are not uncommon today in the theatre. In 1935, and used in combination to form 'a network of vibrations', they were revolutionary for a play billed as a tragedy. Artaud challenged readers of *Le Petit Parisien* to deny that 'repeated sounds have a hypnotic effect'.

In casting, he sought performers who could, as the modern expression has it, take directing. He had written, not a psychological study, but 'an ancient myth' in the guise of a tragedy, which contained 'all the drama of our time in miniature'. Having reserved one of the two big parts, that of Cenci, for himself, he selected for Beatrice a Russian-born society woman, Iya Abdy, who was married to an English lord. Artaud publicly paid tribute to Abdy's 'truly heroic soul', her 'extraordinary power of expression, sense of grandeur', and 'magnificent face that reminds one of the Gorgones of Corfu'. In an article written for *Le Figaro* he even stated that he had written *The Cenci* for her: 'I had met a tragedienne who could yell without swooning – and who grew in strength in proportion with her growing frenzy.' Abdy appears from her photographs to have been a tall, trim, good-looking blonde, probably in her early thirties, who had 'worked with' Dullin, one of Artaud's teachers, for three years. Her fair hair, of shoulder length, would not have been easy to bind to a wheel during the torture scene without straining her neck. Artaud relieved her of that indignity, in any event, by simply tying her wrists to the spokes and draping a rope around her waist. She admired Artaud warmly; and believed in him even beyond the act of faith required for her to take on her first large role on stage and to speak in French, which was not her native language, for she also seems, from some chance remarks in Artaud's letters, to have put up some money.

The roles of Camillo, the Cardinal, and of Bernardo and Giacomo, Cenci's sons, were assigned respectively to Jean Mamy, Yves Forget and Julien Bertheau, all of whom were professional actors, that of Lucrétia, Cenci's second wife, to Cécile Bressant, another professional, while Roger Blin, who later made a reputation for himself as, among other things, Samuel Beckett's foremost director, assisted Artaud with the staging and took on the part, at very short notice, of a deaf-mute assassin. This was his first acting chore.

Artaud himself, his features gaunt, arms stiff, eyes haunted, did not attempt to reproduce Cenci's age, which was nearly twice his own. He looked more like Beatrice's lover than her father, although he may have meant such a relationship to be inferred. He did not spare his already wracked voice. Like the other principal actors, he imbued his movements with the jerkiness of an automaton, presumably in contrast with the animal-mimicking princes, although he did not take it to the extreme he recommended for the two assassins who were supposed to behave like robots. As a further act of depersonalization he placed dummies on stage among the live actors, 'to make the heroes of the play say what perturbs them and what they could not convey in ordinary conversation'. He was trying 'to make beings, rather than men, speak'. Those 'beings' would be 'like great, incarnate forces', yet he felt they would have to remain psychologically plausible.

Now, psychological plausibility was one of the two qualities most of the reviewers missed in the production, the other being conventional diction. Artaud had done his best to prepare them, if not soften them up, for what was to come, with the aid of widespread publicity. On the day of the first performance he was quoted in *Comoedia* as saying that his Cruelty would involve the spectator, who must not be allowed to leave the theatre intact but must be exhausted or even transformed. He added, 'I have tried by all available means to place the audience in the midst of the action.' The failure of audiences and critics to examine Artaud's work on its own merits (and short-comings), or alternatively to resist judging it by conventional standards that did not apply, and their determination to use his own words, like 'tragedy' and 'cruelty', against him – such habits are all too understandable – and current. Few reviews were altogether hostile; most wavered between tolerance and good-natured impatience. Such a reception must have galled Artaud. Open hostility would have been more serviceable to him; against that he might have marshalled some opposition. The play and playing were called melodramatic. Artaud's own acting received no praise whatever; his directing was looked on as being, at best, courageous. Iya Abdy's face and figure came in for some admiration but her Russian accent made her unintelligible to many spectators, and nobody picked up Artaud's suggestions about her truly heroic soul and grandeur. In *La Revue de Paris* François Porché wrote that 'she could have had a brilliant career – in silent films'. The first-night audience, with its heavy sprinkling of society folk, including two genuine princesses, relaxed into laughs through some of the moments of high passion.

The play ran for seventeen days. It should have been the prelude to Artaud's Theatre of Cruelty; it proved to be a substitute for it, an unwished-for consummation. At this remove in time of over sixty years, it is tempting to say that Artaud knew exactly what he wanted from his play but was unable to get it from his collaborators. In other words, that he should have brought in an outside director capable of translating his ideas into a convincing performance. Roger Blin said that Artaud did not have the time to explain his requirements to the actors. He believed they understood him, and so they did, in theory, but they needed guidance in the techniques of presentation that he had in mind.

On the other hand, an outside director would almost surely have distorted Artaud's visions and ambitions. A director's job might be defined as the search for a personal, even oblique, way of bringing somebody else's text to life and the result, given Artaud's temperament, could have been outright disastrous, rather than just commercially unsuccessful. Since Artaud directed no more plays, and his book *The Theatre and Its Double* did not find a wide readership until after his death, the applications of the Theatre of Cruelty were to be left, in any event, to other artists.

CHAPTER 8: ACTOR AND DIRECTOR

1. Artaud also had parts in about twenty films. The ones remembered today are his Marat in Abel Gance's *Napoléon*, his monk Krassien in Dreyer's *The Passion of Joan of Arc*, his youthful beggar in Pabst's *The Threepenny Opera*, and his Savonarola in Gance's *Lucrèce Borgia*. In addition, he played leads in several forgotten films, among them *Tarakanova* and *Gunshots at Dawn* (*Coups de feu à l'aube*).

2. Quotations from essay 'An Affective Athleticism', *The Theatre and Its Double*, pp. 133–141.

3. The interviews with Raymond Rouleau and Tania Balachova, conducted by Randolph Goodman, are included in Dr Goodman's admirable book *From Script to Stage* (New York: Holt, Rinehart & Winston, 1971) in the section that introduces *A Dream Play*, pp. 147–151.

4. This review appeared in *La Gazette du Franc* in June 1928, and is reprinted in part in the *Oeuvres Complètes*, Vol. IV, p. 380. Subsequently, Grémieux was to object to Artaud's writings on the theatre; he threatened to resign from the editorial board of the *Nouvelle Revue Française* unless the editor, Jean Paulhan, refrained from publishing more Artaud. But Artaud went on writing for the *NRF*. See Jean-Louis Brau, *Antonin Artaud*, p. 158.

5. My account of *The Cenci* on stage is taken from a publicity interview from *Le Petit Parisien*, 14 April 1935; an article by Artaud in *Le Jour*, 15 April 1935; another article in *Comoedia*, 5 June 1935; and a collection of reviews, parts of which are

translated into English in *The Drama Review*, T-54, June 1972. Many valuable notes on Artaud's blocking and stage compositions are to be found in the *Cahiers Renaud-Barrault*, November 1965. (Jean-Louis Barrault worked on the production and conducted some rehearsals for Artaud. He has figured prominently in the dissemination of Artaud's ideas. In 1957 he and his wife, Madeleine Renaud, sponsored a collection of essays about Artaud, which were reprinted in 1969.)

Artaud planned, but did not get to realize on stage, a production of Strindberg's *The Ghost Sonata*. His plan is translated into English in *Tulane Drama Review*, T-22, Winter 1963.

9

Social Redeemer

Bernard Shaw prophetically said more than once that the theatre of the twentieth century would go in one of two directions: it would follow Richard Wagner's example of drama with music toward a predominantly sensuous 'total theatre', or it would fall into line with the 'drama of thought', which had acquired its most striking modern forms from Ibsen, and would be variously remodelled by Strindberg, Shaw himself, Pirandello and Brecht. Artaud's Theatre of Cruelty aligns itself more with Wagner than with Ibsen. It is a romantic, evocative theatre of the senses, coloured by dramatic over-statement, and it lacks irony, that favoured device of the intellectual playwright. Although it operates by visual and auditory shock tactics, rather than by the accretion of mellifluous sounds and moods, its extravagance and spell-binding have Wagnerian affiliations.

Joseph Kerman has written that in *Tristan und Isolde*, one of Wagner's largest achievements, the 'fundamental sense is of a progress toward a state of illumination which transcends yearning and pain'.[1] This state of illumination is a passive one. The spectator is played upon, he does not actively seek. Wagner meant to mesmerize his audiences, to immerse them in his flow of 'unending melody'. Nietzsche complained that this '"unending melody" can be clearly understood by comparing it to one's feelings on entering the sea. Gradually one loses one's footing and ultimately abandons oneself to the mercy or fury of the elements.'[2] The spectator may choose to drown in this tide of melody or he may fight back by swimming against it. For Nietzsche, then, Wagner's music lacked a life-giving rhythm. To the older kinds of music, said Nietzsche, one had to dance;

they called forth responsive action. Wagner's led to capitulation. Kerman remarks that the pair of lovers in *Tristan und Isolde* slough off 'all the appurtenances of ordinary existence'. He goes on, 'If this is not to be called a religious experience, it is hard to know what meaning to attach to the term.' Artaud's theatre, too, would swamp its audiences in a religious experience of a sort. Its director is nothing less than an invisible or absent priest who has preordained a communal liturgy. The ideal Artaudian performance thus compares with a traditional service in a house of worship where religious comfort reconciles each congregant with his lot, promising him a spiritual reward in the afterlife for his self-denial in this life. He achieves the promised transfiguration by remaining receptive to the point of passivity, and so discharging his ugly fantasies. His critical faculties, his intellectual misgivings, will be suppressed. He must only believe.

Earlier I mentioned that Artaud's theatre stands at the opposite pole from Brecht's. In an ideal Brechtian performance the spectator receives intellectual signals that keep him alert. He enjoys the emotional conflicts, and may even take sides, but the author's 'alienation-effects' continually break the emotional spell and remind him not to get too caught up in the action. Brecht means him to apply what he is learning from the play to conditions he knows about outside the playhouse in life. This didactic theatre does not openly prescribe remedies for social ills and inequities, but it does foster a critical attitude. In *The Good Woman of Setzuan* Brecht urges the spectator to think about the desirability of change.

Brecht's theatre is reformist, if not revolutionary, in intent. Artaud's is antireformist; it puts on theatre a burden it cannot sustain. By pretending to purge its audiences of their potentially violent 'ideas of war, riot, and blatant murder', by first arousing that violence and then appeasing it, cancelling it out, it substitutes itself for political activity. The Artaudian transfiguration leaves itself open to Brecht's charge against the Aristotelian catharsis: it militates against active social change by inducing a spirit of acquiescence. Artaud evinced some impatience both with political activity and with politically hortatory drama, perhaps because he was tired of the political fulminations he had heard from his one-time Surrealist friends. He had no affection for capitalism, which he thought was 'ready to crack', but came closer to being an anarchist or nihilist than a socialist. In 'Metaphysics and the *Mise en Scène*' he writes, 'Our present social state is iniquitous and should be destroyed. If this is a fact for the theatre to be preoccupied with, it is even more a matter of machine guns.'[3] In saying this he admits that the society-wide peace of mind he dreams of cannot be promoted only from the interior of a playhouse.

Most of the best-known troupes and directors who borrowed from Artaud's theories, among them, the Living Theatre and the Open Theatre, did not lose sight of the Brechtian ideal: theatre that sharpens an audience's political consciousness. Their showings repeatedly levelled political criticism at modern societies. They did not muffle the criticism by processing it through a catharsis.

The trouble with Artaud's diagnosis is that it is deduced from a community that is extremely small, or possibly has a dense network of theatres to accommodate all its public. Just as a people cannot call itself democratic when it is part slave, part free, so a society cannot call itself healthy unless all of its members have undergone healing. There would be no way of testing the efficacy of Artaud's beliefs short of enticing or compelling an entire population to attend the Theatre of Cruelty regularly. Did he think this would be feasible? Quite likely he did. His writings assume that modern society is only the tribe multiplied, with a few added complications of size and crowding. If ritual has helped the one, it should help the other.

Now, if any modern society ever chooses to split up into tribal units, the Theatre of Cruelty will come into its own. It may not achieve everything Artaud wished for, but the gregarious nature of theatre will assert itself and it will make people feel better, and perhaps healthier, as it has already done when tried out by some of Artaud's successors on limited numbers of audiences, rather than on whole communities. In tempering Artaud with Brecht, these artists have demonstrated that the Theatre of Cruelty, which Artaud did not himself accomplish as a codified plan, can be broken down into separable ideas and techniques. As these component parts, Artaud's theories have given the contemporary theatre a series of life-awakening jolts.

CHAPTER 9: SOCIAL REDEEMER

1. Joseph Kerman, *Opera as Drama* (New York: Vintage Books, 1961), p. 195.
2. Geoffrey Clive, ed., *The Philosophy of Nietzsche*, trans. Oscar Levy (New York: New American Library, 1965), p. 291.
3. Artaud, *The Theatre and its Double*, p. 42.

IV

The Legacy as Grab Bag

Artaud in the early 1920s. (© Martinie-Viollet)

Théâtre ALFRED JARRY

VENTRE BRULÉ ou LA MÈRE FOLLE
pochade musicale par ANTONIN ARTAUD
avec la collaboration de MAXIME JACOB

GIGOGNE, par MAX ROBUR

LES MYSTÈRES DE L'AMOUR
par ROGER VITRAC
mise en scène d'ANTONIN ARTAUD
maquettes de JEAN de BOSSCHÈRE

JOUÉS par

GENICA ATHANASIOU
JACQUELINE HOPSTEIN, JEAN MAMY
EDMOND BEAUCHAMP, RAYMOND ROULLEAU
RENÉ LEFÈVRE

les mercredi 1er juin
-- et jeudi 2 juin --
à 21 heures

AU THÉATRE DE GRENELLE
53, rue de la CROIX-NIVERT

MÉTRO : Lignes 5 (Station Cambronne) et 8 (Station Commerce) - AUTOBUS :
X (Vaugirard-Gare Saint-Lazare), Y (Javel-Porte Saint-Martin) - Z (Place Beau-
grenelle-Place Voltaire. - TRAMWAYS : 18 (Porte de Saint-Cloud-Saint-Sulpice),
25 (Auteuil-Saint-Sulpice), 26 (Cours de Vincennes-Mairie du 15e), 28 (Montrouge-
Gare du Nord), 89 (Clamart-Hôtel de Ville).
La location est ouverte au Théâtre de Grenelle et au Théâtre de l'Atelier,
place Dancourt.

An announcement of the first programme at the Alfred Jarry Theatre:
Artaud's Acid Stomach or *The Mad Mother*, Vitrac's *The Mysteries of
Love*, and *Gigogne* by Max Robur (pen-name of Robert Aron), all
directed by Artaud, 1927. (© R. Lalance)

Playbill for Roger Vitrac's *Victor* or *The Children Take Over*. (The play was successfully revived in France and England in the 1960s.) (© R. Lalance)

Cover painting by Gaston-Louis Roux for a booklet issued after the Alfred Jarry Theatre had tried out in four different playhouses, and, finally, closed. The booklet, published in 1930, had a text written jointly by Artaud and Vitrac. It is not known which one of them concocted the title, 'The Alfred Jarry Theatre and Public Hostility'.

The booklet had nine illustrations which, according to the text, were 'not, properly speaking, production photographs…We would rather consider them as a *story without words* [of the Company?] *in nine tableaux vivants* that represent the spirit we tried to uphold. We had a brochure to decorate; we preferred to make up photographs of all our plays which would answer to our intentions, instead of literally reproducing the stagings. The latter were seen, and will be seen again, in the theatre… Antonin Artaud and Roger Vitrac dreamed them up in close collaboration and performed them with Mlle Josette Lusson. The poses and groupings were directed by Antonin Artaud; M. Eli Lotar took the photographs and did the montages.'
(© Mme. J. Colomb-Gérard)

La Société Anonyme
du Théâtre de la Cruauté

La Société Anonyme du THÉATRE DE LA CRUAUTÉ est en voie de formation. Elle sera légalement constituée à partir du moment où un premier capital de **Francs : 100.000** aura été entièrement souscrit.

Dès maintenant, ceux qui désirent s'intéresser à notre entreprise peuvent envoyer à **M. BERNARD STEELE, Éditeur, 19, rue Amélie, Paris (7ᵉ)**, autant de fois la somme de **100 francs** qu'ils désirent souscrire d'actions dans la Société.

M. BERNARD STEELE leur fera parvenir un reçu aux termes duquel il s'engage à verser les sommes ainsi recueillies entre les mains des Administrateurs de la Société au moment de la constitution de celle-ci.

La Société une fois fondée, il sera envoyé aux souscripteurs un extrait des statuts, accompagné du nombre d'actions auquel sa souscription lui donne droit.

Bernard Steel, a publisher, became business manager of the Theatre of Cruelty in 1935 and issued this notice about the formation of a limited company which he and Artaud were convinced would make money.

(© R. Lalance)

Iya Abdy as Beatrice in *The Cenci* (1935), shrinking from her incestuous father. Artaud praised her 'heroic soul' and 'tragic grandeur'. (© Lipnitzki-Viollet)

Beatrice (Iya Abdy), bound to a torture wheel, is asked by Camillo (Jean Mamy) to sign a confession. To the left (between the soldiers) is Lucretia (Cécile Bressant) and on the far-right, Bernardo (Yves Forget). Notice the backdrop, a highly figurative version of a dungeon, which does not attempt to conceal most of the setting from earlier scenes. (© Lipnitzki-Viollet)

Artaud as Cenci: It is hard to decide whether this stance is a still
pose or part of a movement stopped by the camera. The right hand is
slightly blurred, suggesting motion. (© Lipnitzki-Viollet)

10

In the Auditorium

Artaud's theories, which had only a limited currency in the 1930s, had become so voguish by the mid-1960s that critics often bandied them about, and professional theatre people tried to implement them without being aware of their source. As common property, Artaud had joined Ibsen, Stanislavsky, Meyerhold, Pirandello, Brecht and other seminal moderns in the public domain. His ideas were liable to get confused with theirs, or conversely, their ideas were swiped and ascribed to him. The lines of genealogy crossed, recrossed and intertwined. Today it is no longer possible to say that Artaud is purely responsible for many theatrical innovations that identify themselves with the Theatre of Cruelty. Nevertheless, apart from his assertiveness over the director's functions, five Artaudian innovations have found their way, with inevitable modifications, into the artistry of recent directors, playwrights, actors and designers. The first two consist of modernizing the classics and encompassing the audience.

Artaud's call for 'an end to masterpieces' (*'En finir avec les chefs-d'oeuvres'*) went virtually unheeded in 1936 when his essay of that title was published. But the neglect was probably due less to resistance or ignorance on the part of theatre people than to their familiarity with the idea of adapting older plays to a new time and place. Hadn't Terence and Seneca revamped Greek plays to suit Roman tastes? Hadn't the Greek tragedians themselves adapted ancient myths for fifth-century Athenians? Hadn't Shakespeare been a perennially popular subject for face-lifting and more drastic surgery through the eighteenth and nineteenth centuries, from the expurgations of Thomas

Bowdler and the tidyings-up of Colley Cibber to the vaudeville embroideries of Augustin Daly,[1] and on to experiments conducted by William Poel, Harley Granville-Barker and Terence Gray? Hadn't Cocteau modernized *Antigone* in 1922 and *Oedipus Rex* (as *The Infernal Machine*) in 1934? And Eugene O'Neill modernized the *Hippolytus* (as *Desire Under the Elms*) in 1924 and the *Oresteia* trilogy (as *Mourning Becomes Electra*) in 1930? Hadn't Bertolt Brecht rewritten Christopher Marlowe's *Edward II* in 1924, John Gay's *The Beggar's Opera* (as *The Threepenny Opera*) in 1928, Shakespeare's *Measure for Measure* (as *The Roundheads and the Peakheads*), and Corneille's *Horace* (as *The Horatians and the Curiatians*) by 1934?

Artaud was probably taking aim, not so much at integral versions of Shakespeare as at the mummifications of Corneille, Molière and Racine at the Comédie-Française, those 'sacred texts' droningly recited and accompanied by the striking of hallowed, meaningless poses. After World War II critics in other countries recognized similar tendencies: their own classics grew starched through the infusion of too much awe. A classic had made its mark because it challenged its audiences, not soothed them. To muffle the challenges by reverential staging was to destroy the plays.

In England, and later in Canada, Tyrone Guthrie put on vibrant and, for the time, unorthodox revivals, such as a *Troilus and Cressida* set during World War I, with the Trojans wearing British army uniforms and the Greeks, German ones, including uhlan helmets. The Royal Shakespeare Company during the 1960s and 1970s essayed more radical new approaches to Shakespeare, most notably in Peter Brook's *King Lear*, which did away with scenic trappings and reversed the traditional balance of sympathy between Lear and his two older daughters; in Brook's *A Midsummer Night's Dream*, which investigated that comedy's pervasive magic and nightmarishness; and in Peter Hall's and John Barton's *Henry VI*, the three parts of which were remodelled into 'The Wars of the Roses' so as to imply that the British monarchs had found the crown a burden to assume, if not a curse. This theme was later sustained in the RSC productions of *Henry V*, *Richard II* and *King John*. All of these revivals had a cool, impersonal, ceremonial tone that went, one might say, about one-third of the way toward Artaud. Brook, however, did found a troupe-cum-training school named after the original Theatre of Cruelty. The actors, some of whom later went into Brook's celebrated version of *Marat/Sade*, tested out Artaud's *Le Jet de sang*, mouthing abstract noises in place of the spoken lines. One of Brook's associates, Charles Marowitz, went on to do his own adaptations with the Open Space Theatre of *Macbeth*, *Hamlet*, *Othello* and *The Taming of the Shrew*, shaping each play so as to bring out modern elements in the action in a style that conceptually has debts to Artaud.

In New York the Public Theatre and the New York Shakespeare Festival, under the guidance of Joseph Papp, attempted a number of updatings in the late 1960s and after, while relevance was the theatrical catchword. Papp himself directed a *Hamlet* in which the text was cut up and rearranged: the hero spoke his soliloquies in a Puerto Rican accent and in the bedroom scene he perched on a balcony thirty feet above Gertrude dropping peanut shells into her cleavage. This Hamlet was a twentieth-century, metropolitan, alienated Everyman.

In the wake of Artaud, when anything has gone with the classics, should we hold his writings, or their defective reception, responsible for, say, a *Much Ado About Nothing* dumped, with its Italian place names intact, in Spain, or a *Romeo and Juliet* shoved forward a few centuries into the Italian Risorgimento? Some leaps in space and time seem to have been dictated by opportunistic costume designers.

One company that trailed Artaud faithfully was the Performance Group when it transformed Euripides's *The Bacchae* into a partially improvised spectacle, *Dionysus in 69*. The Group, led by Richard Schechner, borrowed primitive rituals of regeneration and fertility from anthropologists' accounts and worked in a set that was textbook Artaud. But by results the most Artaudian revival yet has been Peter Brook's resurrection of Seneca's *Oedipus*. Brook commissioned a new *pointilliste* translation from the poet Ted Hughes, and starred Irene Worth as Jocasta and John Gielgud as Oedipus in an orgy of horrors that led up to Jocasta's punishing herself by sitting on a spike. The audience achieved its catharsis when the cast marched into the auditorium singing, 'Yes, We Have No Bananas', a wildly comic respite. In France Jean-Louis Barrault applied the Artaudian catharsis to a comedy by Molière, whom Artaud once called 'a stupid bastard', at the Comédie-Française, which Artaud once called 'a legalized whorehouse'. Barrault's 1974 version of *Le Bourgeois gentilhomme* ended in a roistering song-and-dance ceremony when M. Jourdain, the hero, was jokingly converted into a high Turkish dignitary, a 'mamamouchi'. The music grew into a frenzied chanting stamping rhythm, almost a rock version of Lully or some other Baroque composer, while the audience, gradually infected by its insistence, joined in the singing and stamping until the staid old Théâtre-Français rang with the noise of actors and spectators performing in unison.

For a show of athleticism entitled *Children of the Gods* and presented in New York by the Shaliko Company in 1973 four Greek plays provided the underpinning. The company ripped chunks of argument and action out of the dramas and set them to improvised movement. The characters had their names stitched on pants or shirts or, in Agamemnon's case, on a life jacket. When not on stage they could be observed in cavelike cubby holes around the arena, dragging at cigarettes, changing costumes, remaking hair styles, draining coffee from styrofoam cups, and shouting choral lines. Above the playing area on four sides there stretched a rectangle of scaffolding equipped with plushy mattresses. Spectators loafed on them, unavoidably becoming the gods who looked down on the proceedings. The actors did not spare their bodies. Two of them might rush toward each other and at the moment when you expected them to thud together with an almighty crashing of bones – they did. Achilles raced around and around like a quarter-miler and did handsprings over two actresses while delivering a soliloquy. Aegisthus hurled Electra to the ground, dived on top of her and pummelled wickedly at her ribs and chest. Orestes thrashed mental initiative, i.e., their imagination. After, and perhaps because of, Barrault's injection of new life into *Bourgeois gentilhomme,* the Comédie-Française leapt into the twentieth century just in time, during its last two decades, with Corneilles, Molières, Racines and Marivauxes that boasted new directors' concepts in abstract settings.[2] Tame overall conclusion: some modernizing isn't bad; some is.

The word 'classics' in recent usage no longer means 'antiques', any more than a 'masterpiece' means 'a great work', only one of an author's best-known writings. We already have 'classics' from well into the twentieth century. Despite the wishes of Samuel Beckett and warnings from his estate, his plays dating back to the late 1950s, which secured their lofty reputations from their non-specificity, have been realized in specific sites or new notions. Joanne Akalaitis situated her *Endgame,* in the New York City Subway. In Deborah Warner's *Rockaby* the sole actor had the temerity to step out of her rocking chair. In a student production of *Waiting for Godot* the four tramps, if they *are* tramps, were played by women as streetwalkers. The 1998 revival of *The Chairs,* directed by Simon McBurney and presented jointly by the Theatre de Complicite and the Royal Court, featured a new translation by Martin Crimp and a novel staging. It showed no recognisable trace of Artaud, but I mention it because a programme blurb described it as 'Ionesco's absurdist classic'. Ionesco wrote it in 1945.

By all odds the most Artaud-drenched production since Artaud's own *Cenci* must have been the stern version of his favourite play *Titus Andronicus,* assembled by Julie Taymor for the Theatre for a New Audience. Taymor, like Artaud, is a highly unorthodox designer. Like Artaud, she has been captivated by the performance arts of Bali, except that she has been there, whereas Artaud saw Balinese art works only at French exhibitions. Somebody (nine named producers, executive producers, co-producers and associate producers, Taymor herself among them) had the pluck to finance a film (title curtailed to *Titus*), which she directed in line with her earlier staging. The chopping-off of several hands and a pair of

111

heads, a variety of stabbings, excision of a tongue, and assorted samples of other unkindness provided streams of artificial gore, acres of sliced, bruised and otherwise abused flesh. How much healthier spectators among the world's markets felt after the dispersal of this film's sumptuous array of images – its processions, body masks and dazzling settings of Titus's and Fellini's and Mussolini's Rome – only the ghost of Artaud may know for sure.

Taymor's film reminds us that Artaud's most conspicuous legacy in AD 2000 is not a theatre of cruelty but a *cinema* of cruelty. In the guardianship of scrupulous artists like Bergman, Kurosawa, Hitchcock and Bresson, the cruelty arouses horror. In high-tech movies that beget car crashes and gigantic globes of flame, grisly nonsense for the sake of special effects, and sustained blank stares by actors to stand in for a language of silence, the cruelty arouses disgust – or gloating. Or laughs. The border between a Cinema of Cruelty and a Cinema of Crudity is hard to discern. We can probably guess at it only by taking into account the calibre of the filmmaker. Granted, any calibre of director, in theatre or cinema, may, from time to time, slip across that border by accident, not by intention, in one direction or the other. But who ever said that criticism is easy at the borderlines – where it counts?

CHAPTER 12: LOOKING BACKWARDS: 2000–1975

1. That the productions in the subsidized theatres cost more than elsewhere, because of handsome premises, advanced technical equipment, elaborate sets, lighting, costumes and expensive leads – stars of national or even international, as opposed to local, fame – doesn't mean that funding came easily. Successive, mostly Tory, governments made life and art unnecessarily ulcerating and precarious for these companies; they had to plead for and eventually rely on large doses of private and corporate support.

2. For further details about the 'nouvelle' Comédie, see Frederick Wiseman's documentary film *La Comédie-Française, ou l'amour*

about in his madness, banging his head, back and heels against what was audibly a hard floor. The number of performances was limited. If the Shaliko performers had thrown in one matinee a week they would have been drawing workmen's compensation. But having chosen the stern material of Greek classics, they were damned if they were going to handle it solemnly. At one point Iphigenia flew up onto the shoulders of Agamemnon. Her face was now on a level with the spectator-gods, and she began to chat affably with them about her impending execution.

Such moments of exchange between actors and audience served as reminders that the indoor theatre prevailing in western Europe after the Renaissance had two interior worlds that were kept apart, a stage and an auditorium. Much criticism has been devoted to the necessity of not letting the reality of the auditorium leak through to the imaginary life on the stage. During the Baroque period, fops in England and France would step right on to the boards during a performance, to the discomfort of actors and audiences. But in general the line between the front of the proscenium arch and the first row of seats in the pit was thought of as an unbreachable border. In the twentieth century the line was broken when the arena or in-the-round stage introduced a new seating arrangement, a central playing area like a boxing ring with aisles leading to its corners, and four quadrants of audience, each of which faced a bank of fellow spectators visible beyond the stage. This type of theatre had returned, in a modified form, to the primitive circle, the natural formation of onlookers surrounding a performance or an event.

Artaud, by mingling spectators and actors in the same space, wanted to envelop both groups in his ritualistic action, to recruit the audience as participants. During the 1960s many smaller companies developed a mania for doing something like this, even when the conditions inside the playhouse were unsuitable. Actors went up and down the aisles, asking spectators questions, sometimes tongue-lashing them, or even physically assaulting them. A seat well off the aisle did not necessarily offer protection. Persevering players, at the insistence of their directors, might squeeze along the rows past people's knees. Or two actors standing in different aisles might carry on a conversation or an argument, like Kabuki performers on parallel, raised *hanamichi* runways, answering each other over the heads of a block of intervening watchers.

This sort of experiment, known as audience participation, for all its occasionally childish or offensive behaviour, had intentions that resembled Artaud's in that it endeavoured to bring the individual spectator into a personal relationship with the individual performer. It was tactile, a reminder that theatre relies on living actors, unlike films and television which display only images of acting. Because they are alive theatre actors are vulnerable; their efforts can be jeopardized, or even halted, by the intervention of the audience. The live performance thus courts continual risks. Certain contemporary dramatists have written plays that emphasize the danger of theatre, among them Arthur Adamov in *Ping Pong* and *Professor Taranne*, and Peter Handke in *Insulting the Public* and *The Ride Across Lake Constance*.

Artaud's plan was more radical than tactile theatre. The audience would sit among the performers, be interspersed in small groups or strung-out lines so that the action went on all round them and they became, in effect, scenic elements. Jerzy Grotowski's Polish Laboratory Theatre played within the confines of its audience's seats. So did the Performance Group. Its production in 1973 of Sam Shepard's *The Tooth of Crime* at the Performing Garage in New York City boasted an environment designed by Jerry Rojo and made up into an array of balconies, platforms and pillars perforated by large holes; these enabled one to watch the show from dozens of vantage points. The actors moved from one portion of the environment to another, while some of the audience followed and others took up new viewing positions.[2]

Joseph H. Dunn staged Fernando Arrabal's *The Automobile Graveyard* in a sort of theatre-in-the-round, a loft the centre of which was occupied by a huge sculpture comprising dozens of parts of wrecked cars welded together. Their headlights, tail lights, directional signals and parking lights provided an irregular tracery of lighting effects. The spectators were led one at a time to their seats in the darkness. When the play began they found themselves in a line of chairs against the four walls; their rectangle of seats defined the playing area. Most of the action took place in the band of floor space between the seats and the junk-car sculpture.

The director Tom O'Horgan once went so far as to reverse the procedure of taking the actors into the auditorium; he took the spectators, singly, into the playing area, thereby also reversing the usual 'balance of power' in the theatre. Instead of one or a few actors confronting an audience of fifty or more people, each spectator 'confronted' a group of actors; he or she was blindfolded by them, led into a room (which became a *pro tem* stage), coaxed to lie down, fondled, and spoken to caressingly. This particular theatre verges on the post-sauna massage or hospital back rub, except that the performance was approximately rehearsed and predetermined. However, its progression would depend in part on the spectator's mood – anger, embarrassment, satisfaction, ecstasy, or whatever – and the responses that mood caused.

The novelties of audience participation eventually endeared it to commercial producers. It was tried in a New York musical called *Dude*, which had a very short run, and then in the revival of another musical, *Candide*, which became a hit by sprinkling its cast, orchestra and audience all over the immense Broadway Theatre, which had been gutted and its upholstered seats replaced by stools and benches so that spectators might feel that they had been casually slumming.

To date the most thoroughgoing abolition of the boundary between actors and watchers must have occurred during *Orlando Furioso*, the Teatro Libero di Roma's dramatization of Ariosto's epic poem. This outsized show, housed in a vast bubble, a kind of geodesic dome, billed itself as 'theatre in the surround', a term that sorts well with Artaud's ideal, even though it was probably coined by the advertising agency that co-sponsored *Orlando Furioso* in the United States. The patrons had no seats. They milled about between two elaborate stages that were set up at either end of the bubble. The open, intervening space was given over to wagons, rather like medieval pageants, which arrived bearing fresh scenes. The audience occasionally had to dodge en masse as new wagons, pushed at breakneck speed by stagehands, came into view from unexpected directions. There was no way to take in the entire performance or to apprehend its sequence, except by consulting the programme notes. Anybody who kept his eyes on these notes, though, was liable to be run down by a wagon. I recall wishing to find a perch somewhere close to the roof for a few minutes during this most thrilling of theatrical events. From there the arena below, with its multiple sets and its spectators moving in waves to avoid the incoming wagons, must have looked like a cross between a fairground and a battlefield.

CHAPTER 10: IN THE AUDITORIUM

1. In 1895 Bernard Shaw wrote: 'The piece founded by Augustin Daly on Shakespeare's "Two Gentlemen of Verona" . . . is not exactly a comic opera, although there is plenty of music in it, and not exactly a serpentine dance, though it proceeds under a play of changing coloured lights. It is something more old-fashioned than either: to wit, a vaudeville. And let me hasten to add that it makes a very pleasant entertainment for those who know no better . . . I cannot feel harshly towards a gentleman who works so hard as Mr Daly does to make Shakespeare presentable: one feels that he loves the bard, and lets him have his way as far as he thinks it good for him.' Bernard Shaw, *Dramatic Opinions and Essays*, ed., James Huneker (New York: Brentano's, 1916), p. 160.

2. Maeterlinck's *Pelléas and Mélisande* was once done in this strolling fashion, but more expansively, while the dramatist was still alive. At his country home, a converted abbey in Normandy, the spectators, carrying camp stools, followed the players from scene to scene into rooms, out on to terraces, and across the grounds of the estate.

11

On the Boards

The remaining three of the five theatrical innovations by Artaud stimulated directors and actors of the 1960s into finding new opportunities to remake contemporary stage life. I would summarize these innovations as using the stage's three dimensions, depersonalizing the characters and inventing new theatre languages.

In the Baroque theatre scenery that incorporated staircases, balconies, or upper-storey windows enhanced an illusion of stage height, but the loftier parts of the set were painted, not built, and could not accommodate actors. Pastorals might feature an occasional god, demon, or humanized monster who flitted by on a wire ten or twelve feet above stage level, or travelled diagonally airborne on a double system of pulleys. Until the twentieth century, though, human performers did not really exploit the stage's height, nor its cubic volume. Height can draw attention to a power relationship, as when one character stands on a superior level to another. It can also enforce isolation, as when a princess is sequestered near the top of a tower. The stage's height and volume, in other words, are more artistically exploited when tall scenic structures are occupied, made animate, than when they are merely decorative.[1]

Artaud, however, wanted to go further than the realistic use of height and volume; he wanted them to serve him fantastically, symbolically. In *The Cenci* Beatrice's being attached to a wheel by strands of her hair pays several theatrical dividends at once. It not only gives the impression, supported in the text, that she has become her own gaoler/prisoner, it also subordinates her to the wheel, underscores her

97

inferiority to it, while her strands of hair, splayed out like the spokes of the wheel, make her look like an impersonation of the torture machinery.

The Living Theatre frequently drew on stage height and volume to create symbolic tableaux, for example the one in *Frankenstein* in which the members of the cast hung together as a human frieze at the back of the stage. Peter Brook sometimes employed scenery with huge sheer surfaces that loomed over the actors and diminished them. In his *A Midsummer Night's Dream* the main action took place within a severe, boxlike, white set designed by Sally Jacobs. Along the top of the box a parapet accommodated other actors who looked down into the enclosed play like a surrogate audience, smiling smugly as though relieved not to be trapped in the nightmare below. There were thus at least two distinct depths of participation for the cast. John Barton's *Richard II* had a balcony representing a turret of Flint Castle; it descended on sloping tracks when Richard was compelled to lower himself by coming to terms with his enemy, Bolingbroke. When he reached ground level, Bolingbroke's soldiers stood behind Richard dwarfing him with their rows of unusually long lances held perpendicular.

Among playwrights, Eugène Ionesco has most resourcefully exploited the stage's volume in the name of fantasy, crowding it with furniture in *The New Tenant*, or showing in *Amédée* a corpse whose giant feet and legs keep growing until they fill one end of the set and then grow out of a window. In *A Stroll in the Air* a character flies away out of sight like a Baroque angel.

The spatial exploration of the acting area helped the theatre to keep pace with the inner-space exploration of modern plays as they ventured into men's and women's psychological hinterland and its landscape of dreams, wishes and fears. At the same time it freed the stage from its old definition as a 'proscenium', or flat surface.[2]

The characters in many recent productions have followed Artaud's prescription and been portrayed, not as psychological entities or collections of human attributes with a unifying past, but rather as symbolic components of the stage picture. In the

98

late nineteenth and early twentieth centuries, Symbolist playwrights like Maeterlinck, the Expressionists in Germany, and directors after Appia, who ushered in the New Stagecraft, wished to bring dramatic characters into an organic harmony with their stage surroundings. An outstanding example of this symbolic harmony is provided by the climactic scene of Strindberg's *To Damascus, Part I*, where the hero, known only as the Stranger, sits in a madhouse facing an assembly of veiled figures, spectral versions of people he believes he has wronged. The tableau forms an animated portrait of the Stranger confronting the sources of his madness. Artaud, who was fascinated by Strindberg's writings, went further than Strindberg in devising characters dominated by the total stage picture. His are governed by outer, as well as inner, forces they do not understand: war, plagues, disasters, social upheaval.

In the contemporary theatre this depersonalizing or unpsychologizing of characters has called for actors trained by methods other than self-recognition. The Open Theatre was started in New York by Joseph Chaikin and Peter Feldman precisely to cope with the roles being written by Beckett, Ionesco and other playwrights for which a conventional training and discipline seemed inadequate. These parts required physical precision and a collective interplay that would more graphically display the symbolic content of the work. The Open Theatre went on to explore another device, inspired possibly by Ibsen's and Strindberg's drama but not by Artaud: multiple-role acting. (In *A Dream Play* and *When We Dead Awaken*, say, several characters may be considered aspects of a larger character; they are parts of a part.) At the Open Theatre one actor would play three, four, or more parts that were not directly interrelated, and would do this by means of transformations, instead of changing costumes and make-up, as has traditionally been the practice with doubling-up of roles. Transformations made possible the genesis of plays such as *Viet Rock* and *Comings and Goings* by Megan Terry, *America Hurrah* and *The Serpent* by Jean-Claude van Itallie, and *Terminal* by Susan Yankowitz, all of them having many roles and scenes. The scenes were not demarcated by curtains, curtain lines, or dramatic changes in the lighting, but by transformations that relied on the skills of the actor. The Open Theatre's training and acting techniques were imitated (sometimes half-heartedly or ineptly) all over the United States, and although the results of transformations owe almost nothing to Artaud, the principles that underlay the training correspond closely to some of the ideas enunciated in Artaud's essay 'An Affective Athleticism' in *The Theatre and Its Double*, in particular the stress Artaud lays on breathing, and on discovering 'points of localization in the body' which are, for him, sources of energy, both physical and psychic. What the new depersonalization amounts to is acting that can imitate thoughts, feelings and still life, as well as human beings. Actors can play chairs, walls, leaves, a tidal wave, rage, success, consciences, feet, noises, or just about anything that can be conceived, abstract or corporeal. Artaud is not intentionally accountable for this development in acting possibilities; it comes more plausibly from several of his contemporaries: Apollinaire, the Surrealists and Cocteau. But his theatrical writings may be applied to an actors' training programme that aims at broadening the scope of the actor's art.[3]

Artaud wanted spoken words delivered, to some extent, for the sake of their sonority, explosiveness, sensuous and associative properties.[4] The playwright who most daringly availed himself of words as suggestive sounds was Ionesco in his earlier plays. Now and then he even breaks a word up into syllables and proceeds to change the vowels and consonants so as to hint at the presence of a baby or small child in the adult who is speaking. The very old couple in *The Chairs* play word games with *on arriva* ('we arrived'), *on a ri* ('we laughed'), and *on a riz* ('we have rice') in the lines:

> Alors on a ri. Ah! . . . ri . . . arri . . . arri . . . Ah! . . . Ah! . . . ri
> . . . va . . . arri . . . le drôle ventre nu . . . au riz arriva . . . au riz
> arriva . . .

Such word play is not quite punning but more like free

association. Of the numerous other playwrights who have contorted words or forced them out of their denotative ruts I will mention only two, Ann Jellicoe and Megan Terry. In Jellicoe's *The Sport of My Mad Mother* a range of sound-values and meanings are checked out when the innocent word 'dolly' is repeated eighteen times, followed by 'shoo' pronounced ten times. In the same play a speech by a character named Dodo consists of fourfold speaking of the words 'no', 'throw', 'so', 'blow', 'crow' and 'doe' – the last line, 'Doe Doe Doe Doe', aurally being the character's own name said twice.

In this extract from Megan Terry's *Comings and Goings* the lines are uttered by a couple 'in bed in early morning':

SHE: Honey?
HE: Arhgghhhh.
SHE: Alarm.
HE: Grrrrrrr.
SHE: Get up.
HE: Uhhhhhhhhhhhh.
SHE: Get up.
HE: Ghhhhhhh.
SHE: Get up.
HE: Fuck it.
SHE: Now now.
HE: Arghhhhh.
SHE: Honey?
HE: OK.
SHE: Honey?
HE: OK.
SHE: Alarm.
HE: OK.
SHE: Get up.
HE: OK.
SHE: Honey?
HE: OK . . . (HE *leaps straight up in the air*.)[5]

As a playwright himself, Artaud used words sparingly and with a certain fastidiousness. As a director, he wanted words to be

101

uttered in unusual ways in order to extend the range of vocal expressiveness. Artaud was unhappy that actors could not scream at full throat; they had 'forgotten how to use their windpipes'. The voice, that versatile instrument, could emit all kinds of untried sounds. If it were pitted against new exercises its owner might learn to produce a flow of literally living sound that was not simply meaningful speech.

Not only playwrights but also contemporary directors have experimented with words as sound. Peter Brook's *Orghast*, performed in Iran, had a text in a new language invented by Ted Hughes. Evidently Brook wanted to unearth a declamatory speech that actors and spectators could believe in as a form of communication but that did not carry hard and fast meanings. Similarly, Brook's *Ik*, which toured villages in Africa, playing outdoors in clearings and not in theatres at all (until it was later repeated in Europe and the United States), was based on tribal speech and intended as a metalanguage, stripped of literary subleties and capable of appealing to people who had no experience of conventional theatre. *Ik* can be viewed as, among other things, an attempt to use theatre for spreading international goodwill and as a harking back to the popular Commedia dell'Arte troupes of the Renaissance and Baroque periods.

In 1975 Brook opened a version of *Timon of Athens* at the Théâtre des Bouffes du Nord, behind one of Paris's largest railroad terminals. The members of his international troupe performed this most intimidating of Shakespeare's dramas in French. The transliteration into another tongue enabled the cast to uncover a new assortment of what Brook called 'musical values' in the text.[6]

In New York the Romanian-born director Andrei Serban had his *Fragments of a Trilogy*, based on three Greek myths, enunciated in ancient Greek or an approximation. Since that language is not spoken today but is only a written remnant with no vernacular accretions, there is no way of knowing how its words were originally pronounced. A modern Greek, for example, could at best follow them haltingly. But Serban, while drawing on an obsolescent tongue, invested his staging with a grandeur and a forcefulness – an unashamed playing out – seldom seem in the theatre since it was dominated by the tics and bashfulness associated with run-down Realism.

For these directors, as for Artaud, vocal sound effects are no more than a fraction of theatre's total language. They take their place in a larger vocabulary that includes mechanical sounds, music and silences; it can then fuse with the language of lights and colour and the language of mime and gesture.

These last two languages, one a responsibility shared by the designer and director, the other shared by the director and actor, have so widely and variously flourished in the past four decades that they have internationalized the theatre in a way that Esperanto could never do for the United Nations. There is no need to state flatly here that lights and colour, mime and gesture, do or do not derive from Artaud. I will take refuge in an overworked metaphor and say that they are part of a tide in which Artaud's ideas are one conspicuous crest. In any event, no advanced director today would dream of embarking on a production without putting a great deal of preparatory thought and effort into his likely deployment of these languages, sound/colour and mime/gesture, for between them these languages constitute what the commercial theatre calls the director's trademark and the non-commercial theatre, his style.

Finally, one must ask what these languages, plus the other innovations, add up to in practice. I would summarize the totality as stage imagery. This is similar to what Cocteau meant by 'poetry of the theatre' or what Vakhtangov had in mind when he wrote of his desire to achieve 'fantastic realism' in theatre, or any one of a number of other ambitions compressed into code words. But Artaud, the prophet whose predictions caught on, must get the principal credit for gaining ground on behalf of stage imagery at the expense of its more successful rival, narrative suspense.

We can get some idea of imagery's new prominence by merely noting some of the images in the plays of three masters of twentieth-century theatre. The heroine of Beckett's *Happy Days*, Winnie, is situated centre stage, buried up to her waist in a mound, and later up to her neck, under a merciless sun. The old man in *Krapp's Last Tape* is divided in an ill-lit den between a tape recorder that has memorialized odd portions of his past and an offstage room where he keeps his whiskey. The two protagonists of *Act Without Words II*, called A and B, crawl out of adjacent sacks. A's movements are 'slow, awkward, absent'; B's are 'brisk, rapid, precise'; both figures are pricked into life by a pointed goad. The three actors in *Play* recite their lines with only their heads showing above three urns; they are galvanized into speaking by a single spotlight that switches from one of them to another. In Ionesco's *The Chairs* an old couple in their nineties are crowded offstage and driven through a pair of windows, the only space left, by tightly packed chairs and an invisible crowd. *Exit the King* gives us an image of monarchy, and of life, in disintegration as King Bérenger more and more feebly totters and crawls about in his throne room until he dies. His kingdom, the idea of his reign, and all remembrance of him as a man and husband die simultaneously. Jean Genet's image of the whorehouse called Le Grand Balcon in *The Balcony* is revealed piecemeal as a series of studios and other theatrical-sounding locations in which the characters act out their fantasies before or beside mirrors and beneath an omnipresent chandelier, that historical token of the indoor theatre. *The Blacks* includes one image that could have been, but probably was not, lifted from Artaud's *The Philosopher's Stone*: a doll-sized puppet is taken from under the skirt of an actress as though a baby were being born.

Artaud's desire to turn a theatre trip into a therapeutic experience has hardly been pursued by other artists, although some doctors and their patients have engaged in psychodramas, which have less to do with theatre than with confessional party games. Insofar as it survives, Artaud's theatre is traceable through technical staging devices, its means, not its ends. The Performance Group in New York adopted more of those means than any other company I have seen, but it lacked Artaud's high seriousness and impassioned commitment. Two of its actors, Spalding Gray and Joan Macintosh, were gifted; the remainder offered agreeable personalities in place of inspiration and accomplishment. Grotowski's Polish Laboratory Theatre, by contrast, was dauntingly accomplished. The actors' faces, especially that of the astounding Ryszard Cieslak, so vividly portrayed moods and sensations that they seemed to paraphrase the actors' entire bodies. But I, for one, felt unable to enter, much less share, the performance with them, and had no sense of the necessity of an audience nor, consequently, any Artaudian catharsis. 'Grotowski knew neither the Théâtre Alfred Jarry nor Artaud's writings,' according to Raymonde Temkine. 'He learned of the existence of Artaud after his death when Grotowski was already the director of the Laboratory Theatre.'[7] Some years ago Grotowski told me more or less the same thing, marvelling that Artaud had been able to speculate so tellingly on the present and the future of the theatre without having had a long-lived company to work with. He, Grotowski, had discovered his own art and begun to realize some of its implications only after a painful period of training and discipline. Undoubtedly Mme Temkine is correct when she concludes that there is no 'close kinship' between Grotowski and Artaud, but, instead, a 'fortunate convergence'.

In the end, Artaud, like Grotowski, is his own man and no more explainable than any other artistic prodigy. He was a natural. He came, he saw and, posthumously, he conquered, but above all, he *saw*. And what he saw opened new perspectives on the stage. Today his poetic ambiguity leaves those perspectives at the mercy of free interpretation. Which is as it should be. More possibilities, more 'impossibilities'.

CHAPTER 11: ON THE BOARDS

1. In the Elizabethan and Jacobean theatre upper levels, especially balconies and galleries, frequently played important parts in organic stage design. Molière is one of the few Baroque playwrights who used scenic height, e.g. in his short farce *The Flying Doctor* and its derivative *George Dandin*.
2. The Greek word *proskenion* originally referred to the front wall

of the *skene*, the actors' changing room and backdrop, or to the columns that subsequently stood immediately in front of that wall. Strictly speaking, the proscenium today should be either the surface of the curtain when it is lowered – although curtains are seldom used any longer – or the forestage that protrudes forward from the proscenium arch, the so-called 'apron'.

3. I do not mean to imply that depersonalized acting is better than character acting; at its finest it extends the actor's capabilities. An actor can give a weak or unimaginative or even unfelt rendition of a chair, while a group attempting to imitate a stream can look like a mudhole.

4. 'Metaphysics and the *Mise en Scène*', *The Theatre and Its Double*, pp. 37–39.

5. This play and certain others of Megan Terry's came out of workshop improvisations with actors. Artaud's rehearsal techniques for *A Dream Play* included improvisation, and not only with words.

    Comings and Goings is published in *Four Plays by Megan Terry* (New York: Simon & Schuster, Inc., 1967).

    The quotations from Ionesco's *The Chairs* come from Eugène Ionesco, *Théâtre*, Vol. I (Paris: Gallimard, 1954), p. 131.

    Ann Jellicoe's *The Sport of My Mad Mother* is published together with *The Knack* (New York: Delta, 1964).

6. For a more detailed description of this staging see Bill Read, 'Peter Brook in Paris'. *Boston University Journal*, Vol. XXIV, No. 3, 1976.

7. Raymonde Temkine, *Grotowski*, trans. Alex Szogyi (New York: Avon Books, 1972), pp. 144–146.

12

Looking Backwards:
2000–1975

Since the preceding chapters were written in the mid-1970s, Artaud's hopes and hoped-for practices have undergone worldwide diffusion and diffusion's inevitable companion, dilution. But even if they are not always acknowledged as his, the very spread and acceptance of his ideas seem to support this book's contention that, as a visionary, he touched many sane practitioners who knew their theatre. The five innovations I associate with Artaud's fervent preachings have continued to percolate into theatre productions, especially those by directors in the second and third generations, who grew up observing performances by the pioneers like Brook, Barrault, Blin, Peter Stein in Germany, and Judith Malina of the Living Theatre in (and out of) the United States.

In Britain, numerous young directors who had tested their aptitudes in fringe theatres or in venturesome troupes outside London won appointments at the Royal Shakespeare Company, the National Theatre and the Royal Court. They included Stephen Daldry, Buzz Goodbody, Nicholas Hytner, Sam Mendes, Simon McBurney, Adrian Noble and Deborah Warner, not all of whom subscribed noticeably to Artaud's styles of theatricality. Brook, Barton, Peter Hall and other senior members of those companies encouraged their younger colleagues to sharpen their skills and juggle much larger budgets.[1] Some of the relative newcomers subsequently became artistic directors of one or another troupe. They took their interpretations overseas, so that London became not only a pre-eminent theatre centre but also a magnet for international theatregoers and a training ground for young critics, performers and graduate students.

In the United States mere contemplation of putting public monies into theatre gives many legislators an attack of the fiscal shudders. Government, federal and local, led by the White House and mayors of deep indifference to the arts in general and of an ignorance too shallow to plumb, cannot conceive of theatre or other cultural endeavours as a social investment. Plays with substance find their stage life for the most part on campus, if anywhere. When they are revived by small, private quasi-professional groups that can hardly afford to splurge on bus fares for the actors, let alone salaries, they come on the scene like shabby, apologetic relatives.

But home-grown, offbeat theatre persists in and out of New York. This miracle defies explanation other than by a hunger to *do* theatre, to plant it and see what comes up. The American Repertory Theatre at Harvard, La Mama in downtown Manhattan, the Public Theatre – part of the New York Shakespeare Festival and named for its founder, Joseph Papp – and the Theatre for a New Audience, which is bent on inducing school children to savour live performances – these, among other experimenters, regularly open themselves to chance.

Encompassing the Audience had moved into the Bigtime well before anyone outside France had heard of Artaud. Night-club comics have long engaged their spectators and begun heated verbal exchanges with a heckler (usually a 'plant') or an embarrassed out-of-towner on the town with a floozie. In an extension of encounters between stage and auditorium, some directors in these post-Artaud days startle audience members by putting actors right into the laps of the opposite sex, not out of mischief alone but also to illustrate interpretations of the play. Actors in a production by Serban have walked or crawled on their knees all the way across a row of thighs. Or taken refuge under a seat in the centre of a row to generate fear, disruption and mirth. Actors in a Gozzi scenario, *The Love of Three Oranges,* have materialized by magic and strode suddenly down the aisles or entered explosively through doors *joué* (in French with English subtitles) and 'No More Playing Safe' by Albert Bermel in *American Theatre,* October 1996, pp. 22–24.

Artaud's Life and Writings:
A Chronology

4 Sept. 1896	Born a Virgo in Marseille, oldest child of Euphrasie Marie-Louise (née Nalpas) and Antoine Roi Artaud, head of a firm that imported textiles, dried fruits and spices from the Middle East. Christened Antonin-Marie-Joseph. Two more Artaud children survived, his sister Marie-Ange and his brother Fernand. Six others died young or at birth.
1901	An attack of meningitis, from which the five-year-old recovered; but severe bouts of head pains followed, and later Artaud developed an intermittent stammer.
1906–14	Attended Collège du Sacré Coeur until age of eighteen.
1910	Published private magazine with some school friends; wrote poems for it under a pen name, Louis des Attides.

*Many of Artaud's non-theatrical writings have been omitted from this summary.

115

1914–15	Recurrent head pains and other ailments. Melancholia. Spent several months convalescing in a sanitarium near Marseille. Opium prescribed for killing the pain. Artaud was to become dependent on drugs and to attempt frequent *désintoxications* in and out of sanitaria during his life.
1916	Drafted into French infantry.
1917	Discharged on medical grounds after nine months of soldiering.
1918	Further institutional treatment for physical and psychological disorders, culminating in a stay of nearly two years at a mental hospital in Switzerland under the supervision of a Dr Dardel. His condition improved, possibly helped by Dardel's encouraging him to write and draw.
1920–21	Went to Paris, at Dardel's suggestion, to get away from home environment. Boarded with Edouard Toulouse, a psychoanalyst with a literary bent. Dr and Mme Toulouse extended Dardel's sympathetic care, giving Artaud the chance to contribute poems to Toulouse's publication *Demain*, to collect some of Toulouse's essays in book form, and write a preface.
1921–24	Aurélien Lugné-Poe, a celebrated director and founder of the Théâtre de l'Oeuvre, gave Artaud his first small part as an actor. Auditioned for Firmin Gémier, another director and one of France's leading actors (Gémier had created the role of Ubu Roi in 1896, the year of Artaud's birth), who sent

him to Charles Dullin.

In Dullin's experimental company, the Théâtre de l'Atelier, Artaud played parts in plays by Molière, Lope de Rueda and Calderón, among other dramatists. He also designed some sets and costumes. Went on to act with the Pitoëffs, Georges and Ludmilla, who produced an international repertory of twentieth-century plays by Blok, Shaw, Pirandello, Leonid Andreyev, Karel Čapek and Ferenc Molnár, in some of which Artaud appeared. His acting career ran parallel with his composition of plays, essays, manifestos and film scenarios.

1923   Wrote short play *The Fountain of Blood* and *Paul the Birds, or The Place of Love*, a 'play in the mind' in the form of a brief scenario featuring Paolo Uccello (Paul the Birds), his wife Selvaggia, Brunelleschi and Donatello, both items forming part of a collection of prose, poetry and drama entitled *The Umbilicus of Limbo*, published in 1925.

1924   Artaud's father died. His mother came to Paris to stay intermittently with him until 1937.

1925   Joined André Breton and the other Surrealists, wrote for their magazine *The Surrealist Revolution*, and edited the memorable third issue.

1922–35   Acted in some twenty films directed by – among others – Abel Gance, Claude Autant-Lara, René Clair, Carl Dreyer, G. W. Pabst and Fritz Lang. His maternal uncle, Louis Nalpas, a film producer and

117

financier, may have helped Artaud with connections and actually getting parts, such as that of Marat in *Napoléon*.

1926–29   With Roger Vitrac and Robert Aron, founded the Théâtre Alfred Jarry in homage to the man generally considered the initiator of the avant-garde drama. The plays, put on at different rented playhouses, consisted of: a) a programme of Artaud's *Acid Stomach, or the Mad Mother*, Vitrac's *Love's Mysteries* and Aron's *Gigogne* (two performances) in June 1927; b) one act of Claudel's *The Noon Divide*, a play the author, who was then French Ambassador to the US, did not want performed – after the performance Artaud publicly denounced him as 'an infamous traitor' – together with a screening of Vsevolod Pudovkin's film *Mother* (one matinee), January 1928; c) Strindberg's *A Dream Play* (two matinees), June 1928; d) Vitrac's *Victor, or the Children Take Over* (three performances), December 1928 and January 1929. The company's fund-raising could not nearly satisfy its ambitious production plans. The casts included Etienne Decroux, later the famous mime theoretician and teacher, Génica Athanasiou, a beautiful actress whom Artaud loved, Tania Balachova, who had the principal role in *A Dream Play*, and Raymond Rouleau, subsequently a theatre and film director. Breton and some companions, who had expelled Artaud from the Surrealist ranks for indulging in the decadence of public theatre, tried to break up one performance; Artaud had them ejected by the police.

Late 1920s and 1930 (dates unsure)	Wrote original scenarios for film shorts: *Eighteen Seconds, Two Nations on the Borders of Mongolia, The Shell and the Clergyman, Thirty-Two, The Butcher's Revolt, Flights*; also a screen treatment for Robert Louis Stevenson's *The Master of Ballantrae*. *The Shell and the Clergyman* was produced and directed by Germaine Dulac, the first woman film director, to whose interpretation Artaud violently objected; at one showing in 1928 he sat in the audience and said audibly that she was 'a cow'.
1930–35	Paid a number of visits to Berlin, sometimes to act in German films, e.g. *The Threepenny Opera*. According to his biographer, Jean-Louis Brau, he discovered there productions directed or inspired by Barnovsky, Piscator, Meyerhold and Reinhardt, 'which strengthened his theories about the theatre'.
1931	Submitted a 'talking pantomime' *The Philosopher's Stone*, together with a production plan for Strindberg's *The Ghost Sonata*, to Louis Jouvet, one of the two best-known pupils of Jacques Copeau (the other was Charles Dullin, with whom Artaud remained friendly). Through most of 1931 and 1932 Artaud persisted in trying to make a place for himself in Jouvet's troupe; he read manuscripts, poured out suggestions, begged to be given a play to stage or to work on a production with Jouvet.
Witnessed the Balinese theatre at an international (colonial) exposition in Paris. This was the second such exposition he had attended, but it made a stronger impression

on him than the first one, which he saw during a visit home to Marseille in 1923.

1931–32   Wrote theatrical scenario *There is No More Firmament* dealing with a cosmic catastrophe. According to the editor of Artaud's *Oeuvres Complètes*, this, like other compositions of Artaud's, was probably dictated, rather than written by hand.

1933   Drew up an outline of a four-act play *The Conquest of Mexico*, published in part later in *The Theatre and Its Double*.

1934   Published his *Heliogabalus, or the Anarchist Crowned*, a prose study of the tyrannical Roman emperor.

1935   Inaugurated the 'Theatre of Cruelty' which he had been thinking about and planning for since 1932. He had had fallings-out seven years before with Robert Aron and Roger Vitrac, his partners in the Théâtre Alfred Jarry. This time he wanted to go it alone. In choosing the name Cruelty, Artaud turned down the suggestions of friends for such less harsh titles as Theatre of Becoming and Theatre of the Absolute. He mounted a production of his own play *The Cenci* at the Folies-Wagram Theatre. It opened on 6 June, collected unappreciative notices, and ran for two and a half weeks, after which the Theatre of Cruelty was dissolved. He declined an offer, later in June, to collaborate with Jean-Louis Barrault. Took a ship to Mexico by way of Cuba; lectured at the University of Mexico three times; wrote some newspaper articles.

Leaving Mexico City, he struck north into mountainous country to find and stay among the Tarahumara Indians. Took part in an initiation ceremony, sampled the sacred peyote, and witnessed a rite of transfiguration that overwhelmed him and seemed to confirm many of the beliefs about rituals expressed in his previous writings.

1937   Back in Europe he became engaged to a young Belgian woman, Cécile Schramme. Embarked on two attempts in drug clinics to break his addiction; neither was successful.

Went to stay in Brussels with Cécile's family. While there he gave a public lecture at which he lost control, insulting the audience and himself. Engagement broken off by Cécile's father.

Published a pamphlet *The New Revelations of Being*, which predicted that fire would consume the world in November of that year.

August: went to Ireland to seek the 'last authentic descendants of the Druids . . . who know that . . . humanity must disappear by water and fire'. Subdued by Irish police and forcibly shipped back to France. Put in a straitjacket after an incident on board. At Le Havre Artaud was confined to an asylum.

1938   Collection of Artaud's essays in book form, *The Theatre and Its Double*, a title he had dreamed up during his voyage to Mexico. Most of the essays had originally consisted of lectures at the Sorbonne and elsewhere during the previous seven years.

Late 1937–43	Was held successively in four asylums in northern France. The war and the German occupation made it difficult for friends to assist Artaud for a time. Alternating spells of lucidity and schizophrenia. Conditions in the asylums may have aggravated Artaud's illness.
1943	Thanks to the efforts of Robert Desnos, the poet, Artaud was transferred to Rodez asylum in the south, under the care of Dr Gaston Ferdière who, with the most humane intentions, administered electric shocks. Artaud dreaded this treatment, but whether it helped him or whether he made some spontaneous, or willed, recovery, he took up his writing and drawing again, and completed the abandoned manuscript of his *Travel to the Land of the Tarahumaras*, published in 1945.
1945	Friends visited Artaud fairly regularly at Rodez.
1946	A group of distinguished contemporaries secured his release from Rodez, against the wishes of his mother and sister. A benefit reading of his poetry by big-name actors, and a sale of drawings and papers, raised money for his upkeep. He went to a rest home in Ivry on the outskirts of Paris and lived there in a two-room pavilion. Gaston Gallimard proposed a complete edition of Artaud's works. Artaud wrote a preface to this edition before the contract was signed. The first volume, containing the preface, would not be published for another ten years.

1947	Won the Sainte-Beuve Prize for an essay, 'Van Gogh, Society's Suicide'. (In 1960 Jean Hort adapted the title for a biography of Artaud: *Antonin Artaud, Society's Suicide*.) Gave a public reading at the Vieux Colombier (Copeau's old theatre) of his recent poems to an over-capacity audience.
	Commissioned by the Radiodiffusion Française to write a radio script. *To Put an End to God's Judgment*, recorded for a select audience of French luminaries, was denied a public broadcast and said by one official to be obscene. Protests by Artaud and members of the private audience were unavailing.
4 March 1948	Artaud died of rectal cancer. He had been in agony for months; his doctor, who had diagnosed the cancer as terminal, had allowed Artaud to take all the drugs and sedatives he needed to numb the pain.
5 March 1948	Artaud's second life begins.

Selected Bibliography

BOOKS (IN ENGLISH)

Antonin Artaud: Collected Works. Edited by Victor Corti. Translated by various writers. London: Calder & Boyars, 1968. The volumes that have appeared at this writing include many of Artaud's most celebrated writings, but do not by any means reproduce all the French material.

Artaud, Antonin. *The Theatre and Its Double*. Translated by Mary Caroline Richards. New York: Grove Press, 1958.

Esslin, Martin. *Antonin Artaud*. London: Penguin, 1976.

Greene, Naomi. *Antonin Artaud: Poet Without Words*. New York: Simon & Schuster, Inc., 1970.

Hirshman, Jack, ed. *Artaud Anthology*. San Francisco: City Lights, 1965.

Knapp, Bettina. *Antonin Artaud: Man of Vision*. New York: David Lewis, 1969.

Sellin, Eric. *The Dramatic Concepts of Antonin Artaud*. Chicago: University of Chicago Press, 1968.

Sontag, Susan, ed. *Antonin Artaud: Selected Writings*. New York: Farrar, Straus & Giroux, 1976.

PERIODICALS AND ARTICLES

The Drama Review, T-54, June 1972. Material on *The Cenci*.

Tulane Drama Review, T-22, Winter 1963. Some of Artaud's writings, plus critical articles by Paul Arnold and Romain Weingarten.

Brook, Peter. 'Artaud for Artaud's Sake'. *Encore*, May–June, 1964.

Caws, Mary Ann. 'Artaud's Myth of Motion'. *French Review*, February 1968.

Chiaromonte, Nicola. 'Antonin Artaud'. *Encounter*, August 1967.

Goodman, Paul. 'Obsessed by Theatre'. *The Nation*, November 29, 1958.

Hivnor, Mary Otis. 'Barrault and Artaud'. *Partisan Review*, March 1958.

Kitchin, Laurence. 'The Theatre of Cruelty'. *The Listener*, 19 September 1963.

Koch, Stephen. 'On Artaud'. *Tri-Quarterly*, Spring 1966.

Marowitz, Charles. 'Notes on the Theatre of Cruelty'. *Tulane Drama Review*, T-34, Winter 1966.

Marowitz, Charles. 'Artaud at Rodez'. *Theatre Quarterly*, No. 6, Summer 1972.

Saillet, Maurice. 'Close to Antonin Artaud'. *Evergreen Review*, May–June 1960.

Seymour, Alan. 'Artaud's Cruelty'. *London Magazine*, March 1964.

DISSERTATIONS

Nash, John Richard. *Jarry, Reverdy, and Artaud: The Abrupt Path.* Stanford University, 1967.

Tembeck, Robert Edward. *Antonin Artaud and the Theatre of Cruelty.* University of Minnesota, 1965.

BOOKS (IN FRENCH)

Antonin Artaud: Oeuvres Complètes. Paris: 1956. Gallimard has so far published eleven volumes, plus a supplement to Volume I and a separate collection of Artaud's letters to Génica Athanasiou. In addition, a 'new, revised, and corrected edition' of the complete works has begun to appear.

Armand-Laroche, Jean-Louis. *Antonin Artaud et son double.* Périgneux: Fanlac, 1964.

Bonneton, André. *Le Naufrage prophétique d'Antonin Artaud.* Paris: Lefebvre, 1966.

Brau, Jean-Louis. *Antonin Artaud*. Paris: La Table Ronde, 1971.

Charbonnier, Georges. *Antonin Artaud*. Paris: Seghers, 1959, 1970.

Hahn, Otto. *Portrait d'Antonin Artaud*. Paris: Le Soleil Noir, 1968.

Hort, Jean. *Antonin Artaud: le suicidé de la société*. Geneva: Editions Connaître, 1960.

Joski, Daniel. *Antonin Artaud*. Paris: Editions Universitaires, 1970.

Sollers, Philippe, ed. *Artaud*. Paris: Union Générale d'Éditions, 1973. Lectures and discussions from a cultural conference held in 1972 at Cerisy-la-Salle.

Tonelli, Franco. *L'Esthétique de la cruauté*. Paris: 1972.

Virmaux, Alain. *Antonin Artaud et le théâtre*. Paris: Seghers, 1970.

PERIODICALS AND ARTICLES

Cahiers de la compagnie Madeleine Renaud–Jean-Louis Barrault. Paris: Gallimard, 1969. Special issue, 'Artaud et le théâtre de notre temps', a collection of critical essays and memoirs, first published in 1957, reprinted in book form 1958, reprinted and enlarged, 1969.

84. Special issue devoted to Artaud, 1948.

France-Asie. Special issue. 'Hommage à Antonin Artaud'. September 1948.

K. Special issue devoted to Artaud, 1948.

La Tour de Feu. Special issue. 'Antonin Artaud ou la santé des poètes'. December 1959.

Gide, André. 'Hommage à Antonin Artaud'. *Combat*, May 19, 1948.

Grotowski, Jerzy. 'Il n'était pas entièrement lui-même.' *Les Temps Modernes*, April 1967.

Mallausséna, Marie-Ange (Artaud's sister). 'Antonin Artaud'. *La Revue Théâtrale*, 1953.

Nordmann, Jean-Gabriel. 'Antonin Artaud et le surréalisme'. *Europe*, November–December, 1968.

Prével, Jacques. 'En compagnie d'Artaud'. *La Nouvelle Revue Française*, March 1962.

Roy, Claude. 'Le Théâtre de la cruanté en Europe'. *La Nouvelle, Revue Française*, May 1965.

Scarpetta, Guy. 'Brecht et Artaud'. *La Nouvelle Critique*, June 1969.

DISSERTATIONS

Liéber, Gérard. *Antonin Artaud, homme de théâtre*. University of Paris, 1967.

Novarina, Valère. *Antonin Artaud, théoricien du théâtre*. University of Paris, 1964.

Zorilla-Velasquez, Oscar. *Antonin Artaud, théoricien et technicien de l'art dramatique*. University of Montpellier, 1966.

Peter Lacey, *The Compagnie* ... *Les nouvelle Revue française*, March 1962.

Eric Glasgow, *Le Théâtre de Bernard-Marie Koltès* ... *Nouvelle revue française*, May 1990.

Benedict Clare, *Theatre* ... *La Nouvelle Critique*, June 1969.

Index

N.B. The writings of Artaud are entered alphabetically under his name. Names of characters are not indexed, only the plays in which they appear.

131